HOPE IS THE THING WITH FEATHERS

AND TWO OTHER SHORT PLAYS

BY RICHARD HARRITY

PREFACE BY EDDIE DOWLING

★

DRAMATISTS
PLAY SERVICE
INC.

PREFACE

In this collection of short plays Richard Harrity, who has been hailed by the critics and the public as an exciting and original new talent in the American theatre, presents a vivid and dramatic cross-section of some lesser known aspects of life in that modern Babylon called New York City. For example, in *Hope Is The Thing With Feathers* he probes the illusions and hopes of a group of derelicts spending the night in a pavillion in Central Park. Writing with insight and understanding, Harrity has created a beautiful and moving play out of the attempts of a band of vagabonds to snare a duck for their dinner in a nearby lake. You will alternately laugh and cry at the characters in *Hope Is The Thing With Feathers*, and, I affirm, be reminded that hope burns bright even in the sorriest of men.

When I first saw this play enacted by a group of actors called The Six O'Clock Theatre under the auspices of the Experimental Theatre, I recognized a new talent and determined to accept the challenge of presenting an evening of Harrity one-acters on Broadway.

The second play, *Home Life of a Buffalo,* is a special favorite of mine. It is a compelling tragic comedy of a dancer who stubbornly refuses to admit that vaudeville is dead. Ray Dooley, my wife, who returned to Broadway after being away from the stage for fourteen years to star in this play with me, shares my belief that this is the truest and most honest picture of small-time vaudevillians ever written. And, I hasten to add, we know whereof we speak, because before Ray Dooley became a great Ziegfeld star, and before I started producing, directing and acting in such dramas as Paul Vincent Carroll's *Shadow and Substance*, William Saroyan's *The Time of Your Life*, Tennessee Williams' *The Glass Menagerie*, Eugene O'Neill's *The Iceman Cometh*, etc., we, ourselves, were small-time vaudevillians. *Home Life of a Buffalo* is, therefore, very close to our hearts and will, I am confident, entertain and move any audience with a heart.

3

The third play, *Gone Tomorrow,* is a hilarious study of an Irish-American family waiting for an aged uncle to die so that they can divvy up whatever money he might have saved. The aged uncle, however, is a contrary old Harp who vehemently declines to go on his last journey until he is darn good and ready. Harrity's knowledge of the Irish enables him to write a rib-tickling comedy that is in the best Abbey Theatre tradition.

When I produced these plays on Broadway last season under the overall title of *Hope's the Thing,* Harrity's fresh and original treatment of his material presented a challenge to me as a director and as an actor. I felt that here was a new playwright who had an exciting way of making his dramatic statements. After studying the plays, I believed that they would benefit through a fresh approach, and I decided to dispense with formal scenery in presenting them. In other words, we used only essential props, presented the plays on a bare stage and urged the audience "on your imaginary forces work." The audience responded so well that many people came to me afterwards and asked who did the "sets." Others, carried away by the originality of the plays and the acting, actually described the nonexistent sets to me. In short, the audiences who saw these plays reaffirmed the theatre's oldest truism, "the play's the thing."

Actors and directors, whether they be amateur or professional, will, I am sure, be stimulated by the challenge and the excitement inherent in these plays by Harrity, and will, perhaps, agree with me that they can best be presented on a bare stage, without scenery. If you agree with this assumption, all that is needed is a narrator to "set" the stage and to explain where imaginary doors, windows, etc., are supposed to be, and the audience will cooperate and upon their "imaginary forces work."

But regardless of how *Hope Is The Thing With Feathers, Home Life of a Buffalo* and *Gone Tomorrow* are produced, with or without scenery, they will provide a rich and exciting evening by an original and very talented new playwright.

EDDIE DOWLING

HOPE IS THE THING WITH FEATHERS

CHARACTERS

OSCAR	SWEENEY
DOC	CHARLIE
STEVE	OLD MAN NELSON
WILER	JOE
MAN	

(Scene: A summer-house in Central Park. It is a pavillion-like structure with several vertical logs supporting the roof. A semicircular bench topped by a rustic railing runs across the entire upper part of the stage. There is an entrance L. and another R. In the opening between the railing and the roof, lights show here and there, indicating several tall buildings in the distance. Bright moonlight pervades the scene, giving it a penny-postcard prettiness. From far off is heard a boat whistle, distinct and long-drawn-out, followed by the clop-clop of a horse on pavement; the sounds of several automobile horns from various distances; a trolley-car rumbling over tracks; and, finally, the quack-quack of ducks in the nearby lake.

Standing at the R. entrance is OSCAR, a rather well dressed man of medium height. He is thirty-seven. At first glance he might be taken for a nearby apartment dweller out for a stroll. He studies the scene for a moment, then carefully inspects the bench. Selecting a spot he dusts it with a handkerchief, then removes his coat and puts it down. He stands with his arms wrapped tightly around himself as though trying to stop his shivering, then takes a newspaper and slides it inside his shirt. He puts another newspaper on top of his shirt, gets back into his coat and sits down on bench. He pulls up his trousers, wraps a newspaper around each leg, readjusts trousers and finally stretches out. Three other men, barely discernible, are also stretched out on bench.

6

They are: DOC, *a small, weazened, bandy-legged man of fifty-five, wearing an overcoat and a stocking cap pulled down over his ears;* STEVE, *forty-eight, a medium-sized man who walks with a slight limp; and* WILER, *forty-five, who is curled up like a ball in an overcoat several sizes too big for him.*

For a moment they are all quiet, then WILER *begins to twist and squirm. Suddenly he jumps up and tests bench with both hands as one might a bed. He reverses his position, but gets right up again and angrily adjusts his overcoat. He stretches out again, this time on his back, is calm for a second, then sits up, stares off at the buildings and violently shakes his fist at them.)*

WILER. *(Half to himself)* Never knowed it to fail.

STEVE. *(Raising his head)* Hey, how about a little quiet?

WILER. Go to hell. (WILER *stretches out again and they are all quiet for a while. Then* DOC, *who has begun to cough convulsively, sits up.* WILER *also sits up—glares at* DOC, *then suddenly goes into an exaggerated fit of faked coughing.)*

WILER. *(Viciously, to* DOC) How do you like that? *(Curls up on bench again.)*

OSCAR. What's eating him now? *(*DOC *shakes his head.)* He must think he owns this park. *(As* DOC *continues to sit, the quack-quack of the ducks is heard again.* DOC *listens, then getting up he walks over to* R., *and, leaning on railing, looks off into the night.* STEVE *raises his head and watches him.)*

STEVE. What are you looking at?

DOC. *(Startled)* Nothing.

STEVE. You're lying.

DOC. No, I ain't, Steve.

STEVE. Then what are you looking at?

DOC. *(After a pause)* Well, I was kind of looking at the ducks.

STEVE. The ducks. I might of knowed it. Ducks.

DOC. *(Becoming excited)* Steve, I never seen so many ducks. The lake's full of them. I count twenty-four in one bunch before. Fat ones.

STEVE. Ducks. *(Suddenly suspicious)* Is that why you drag me up here?

DOC. Listen, Steve, I got them ducks all figured out.

STEVE. When we was down at the Battery last week it was

eels. You had them all figured out too, didn't you? *(Imitating* DOC) 'All the eel does, Steve, is bite on the silk thread and he can't let go . . .'

DOC. But ducks is different.

STEVE. Will you shut up about 'em?

DOC. All right, Steve. But you're making a mistake.

STEVE. *(Starting to get sore)* Shut up, I said. (SWEENEY, *a tall, lanky man around forty, wearing raincoat, derby, pair of sneakers, enters from R. and starts to stretch out on bench. He is followed immediately by* CHARLIE. *The latter is a small, wiry man with a broken nose and a cauliflower ear which stamp him as an ex-pug. He is fifty-seven.* CHARLIE *watches* SWEENEY *as the latter arranges himself on bench, then bursts out laughing.* CHARLIE *laughs so hard he has to grab one of the logs for support.)*

CHARLIE. *(Gasping for breath)* I'll split a gut. *(Laughs again)* Me eyes must be sure getting bad. I been folleying dis Willie since he come in de park. *(Again he laughs)* Oh, Christ, I bet I split anudder gut . . . an' I'm jist gointa put de bite on him an' . . . *(He laughs again)* He's carrying de banner too, fer Christ sake. Now, how do yuh like dat? *(He starts laughing again and* SWEENEY *watches him as he hangs on to the log with one hand and slaps it with the other. Finally* SWEENEY *breaks into a grin, then joins in* CHARLIE'S *laughter.)*

OSCAR. What the hell is this, the fun house at Coney Island?

STEVE. I bite. (CHARLIE *stops laughing, walks over to bench and sits down.)*

CHARLIE. If I don't stop, I'll split anudder gut. *(Ducks are heard quacking again, and* DOC *sits up.)*

DOC. Hear 'em? Hear 'em?

SWEENEY. It's a great night for ducks, ain't it?

DOC. Is there a lot of ducks there when you come by?

SWEENEY. I don't see the water for the ducks. The lake's covered with them.

DOC. Do you hear what he says, Steve? The lake's covered with ducks. He can't even see the water. That's what I been trying to tell you.

STEVE. *(Grabbing* DOC) I don't want to hear about the ducks. *(Shakes* DOC *violently, then shoves him down on bench)* Now will you shut up about the ducks?

SWEENEY. Quack-quack, quack-quack. *(Rapid footsteps heard offstage and* OLD MAN NELSON *appears. He is hatless and wears an overcoat faintly resembling a patchwork quilt. He has a snow-white beard and a long shock of white hair. He could be any age from sixty to a hundred. When he talks he chuckles continually. He trots over to bench and heaves a great sigh of relief as he plumps down on it.)*

OLD MAN NELSON. Oh, boy, what a relief sitting down is. My feet was killing me. Both of them. I been going and going and going all day like there was somebody after me. Once I'm scooting along so fast I stop and ask myself—'Where's the fire? What are you rushing for? *(Chuckling)* I guess I was just trying to keep up with everybody else. *(Stops talking, looks around bench; then addressing no one in particular)* This ain't a bad turn-out for a night like this.

SWEENEY. I bet nobody was following him.

CHARLIE. If dey was, it's dere own fault.

OLD MAN NELSON. Say, this park's so cozy I wonder I never sleep here before. I think I'm going to like it fine. It's every bit as good as the Battery.

OSCAR. The Battery ain't so bad.

OLD MAN NELSON. Oh, the Battery's a great place—in the summertime. There's always something going on. Ships going and coming and all kinds of hustle and bustle. Say, was you ever down there at noon, when people come out of the buildings and feed the pigeons? My, that's a sight, ain't it?

OSCAR. If only they don't blow them horns all night.

OLD MAN NELSON. I got so I don't mind 'em at all. Every time I hear a horn I try to think where the boat's going and wish I was going along myself. Say, was you ever over to Carl Schurz Park on the East River? There ain't so much hootin' and tootin' over there.

STEVE. If you was to pay me, I won't sleep in the Battery any more.

OLD MAN NELSON. I like all the parks. I ain't seen one yet I don't like.

STEVE. Bryant Park is another one I won't sleep in any more. I cork off there one night and some bastard steals a good pair of shoes right off my feet.

OSCAR. I tell you where you don't have to worry about your shoes—Gramercy Park. They don't let you sleep in it.

OLD MAN NELSON. I sleep in Gramercy Park once. I follows a lady with a go-cart in and I don't come out again; and I sleep in Independence Square in Philly; and I sleep in Potomac Park in Washington; in Fountain Square in Cincy. And I sleep up in the Boston Common, and they are all fine. I like them all. *(Chuckling)* I once sleep for a week down in Virginia in a park, and what do you think they calls it—'Hungry Mother Park'. Now ain't that a good one—'Hungry Mother Park'.

CHARLIE. *(To* SWEENEY*)* He oughta be in de nut house—'Hungry Mudder Park'.

OLD MAN NELSON. Oh, and don't forget Madison Square. Now, there used to be a place. What a park that was in the old days, when the Garden was down there. Oh, the horse-cars and the carriages with the swells in 'em. And all the pretty ladies. And the nights they used to have the fights. I never seen such crowds. And the people coming out of the shows, too. Oh, what a sight for sore eyes that was. *(Proudly)* Why, I was sleeping there the night Harry Thaw shoots that other fellow. *(Chuckling)* But I guess that's all before your time.

CHARLIE. *(Becoming belligerent as he goes along)* What t'hell yuh know about Madison Square? Yuh old billy-goat. I know more about Madison Square then yuh'll ever know an' I ain't no goddam bum, seester? I fight in de Garden, when it is de Garden—me, dis gie yuh're looking at. An' many's de time, agin some of de best punks to come up de pike. An' dey don't lay a hand on me, what do yuh t'ink dat?

OSCAR. *(Looking at* CHARLIE's *battered face)* What happened, did the roof fall on you?

CHARLIE. *(Turning on* OSCAR*)* I say, dey never lay a hand on me, and yuh don't lay a hand on me now, yuh lousy bastard.

OSCAR. I don't want to lay a hand on you. (CHARLIE *yanks a handkerchief out of his pocket, spreads it on the ground and stands on it.)*

CHARLIE. An' I don't move offen dis noserag.

SWEENEY. I see Young Griffo do that once.

CHARLIE. Yuh're a liar. Yuh never seen Young Griffo do dis on a noserag dis size in yuh're life. *(Then to* OSCAR, *with calm belief in himself)* Now jab me, yuh punk, and if you got four arms, yuh don't lay a hand on me.

OSCAR. I got nothing against him.

SWEENEY. You ain't going to hit him—is he?

CHARLIE. How de hell's he gointa hit me?

SWEENEY. Go ahead an' jab him. (SWEENEY *pushes his fist out slowly to demonstrate how it is to be done.* OSCAR *follows suit just as slowly.)*

CHARLIE. *(Furious)* I kin duck that if me neck was broke! Goddam it, come on an' jab me. Jab me. (OSCAR *hesitates a moment and then quickly jabs at* CHARLIE—*before the latter has time to duck. The blow catches him square on the nose and sends him sprawling.)*

OSCAR. Geez, I don't mean to do that, buddy. I got nothing against you.

CHARLIE. What de hell yuh beefing about yuh lousy bastard? Yuh want me to give yuh somet'ing to beef about? Me foot slips, fer Christ sake.

SWEENEY. You oughta use a bigger rag—like Young Griffo uset to use.

CHARLIE. Yuh jist mine yuh business, punk, or I'll fix it so yuh won't have any to mine.

OSCAR. *(Who has picked up handkerchief)* Here you are, pal.

CHARLIE. Don't do me no favors. I kin pick it up meself. *(Then to no one in particular)* Me foot slips, fer Christ sake. (WILER, *who has been stretched out on bench, suddenly sits up and shakes his fist at the buildings again.)*

WILER. Why don't it go out?

OSCAR. What the hell are you yipping about now?

WILER. I'll tell you what I'm yipping about. Night after night that goddam light—the ninth floor up and the third window in—it never goes out.

STEVE. If the light shines in your eyes, why don't you move?

WILER. Yeah! Sure! Why don't I move? Ain't I got any rights? Why don't it go out?

CHARLIE. *(To* SWEENEY) Anudder gie with bats in the belfry.

SWEENEY. The joint's lousy with 'em.

OSCAR. *(Who has been looking around)* This ain't the best park in town. Give me the Bronx Park.

STEVE. Them animals in the Bronx Park don't let me sleep. I always worry they're breaking loose.

SWEENEY. I always worry about the stink.

OSCAR. What about the animals they got here—don't they stink?

SWEENEY. *(Snickering)* No; they just smell bad.

OSCAR. *(Getting sore)* They ain't got any them damn seals in the Bronx Park. ·

WILER. *(Sitting up)* The only time you ever hear the seals here is when they're feeding 'em.

OLD MAN NELSON. Golden Gate Park out in Frisco is the place for seals. I never see so many of 'em. They'll come right up and eat out of your hand.

STEVE. *(Who has been thinking)* If you get over by the Botanical Gardens there ain't no stink.

SWEENEY. No wonder they stole his shoes. *(Quack-quack of the ducks is heard again and* DOC *jumps up. He starts yanking string, weights, and other junk out of his pockets onto bench.* STEVE *gets up and moves over toward* DOC *menacingly.)*

DOC. *(Excited)* Steve, I know we can get one this time. Give me a hand here.

STEVE. *(Grimly)* I warned you.

DOC. *(Stamping his foot)* But the lake's covered with 'em. Don't he just say so? (STEVE *leaps at* DOC *and grabs him by the throat.)*

DOC. *(Gasping for breath)* Leave me go, Steve. You're hurting me. Leave me go.

OSCAR. *(Jumping up and grabbing one of* STEVE'S *arms)* Leave him go. *(Then quickly to* OLD MAN NELSON) Get his other arm. (OSCAR *and* OLD MAN NELSON *pull at* STEVE'S *arms and yank him away from* DOC.)

STEVE. Let go of me, goddam it; let go of me.

CHARLIE. Leave 'em go at it. Dey can't whip dere weight in creampuffs.

DOC. I can't be wrong all the time, Steve.

STEVE. *(Fighting to get at* DOC) Let go of me. I'm going to kill the bastard this time.

OSCAR. He ain't done nothing to you.

STEVE. He's making me blow my top—that's what he's done to me. I been with him six weeks and he's after everything. He has me behind a tree knocking two sticks together till my arms ache. He says that's the way we can get a squirrel. Then

he has me dunking for eels with a silk thread till I'm dippy
Why he's even after seagulls. The son of a bitch is crazy!

DOC. *(Appealing to others)* But I been catching things all my
life.

STEVE. You been trying to catch 'em.

DOC. *(Earnestly)* I catch gophers with just a piece of string
. . . and I can catch crabs . . . and I catch rabbits . . .
and I can get one of them ducks in the lake. I got it all figured
out. I ain't crazy.

SWEENEY. *(Snickering to CHARLIE)* He thinks he's Frank
Buck.

CHARLIE. Anudder one of 'em. *(Turning and looking at OLD
MAN NELSON)* 'Hungry Mudder Park'.

DOC. Listen, fellas, I admit I been wrong sometimes. Everybody makes mistakes. But I ain't crazy, and I can get one of
them ducks. . . . There's ducks in the lake, ain't there? It's
covered with 'em. Big fat ones. Don't everybody like duck?
Could you put a better thing in your belly? Well, I know I
can get one of 'em. Is that crazy? *(Becoming excited)* Look,
I got it all figured out. I'll prove I can get one of 'em. Watch
this . . . *(Fishes in his pocket and pulls out some other
junk, which he puts on bench.)*

STEVE. I'm warning youse; he's going to get you worked up
like he gets me worked up. *(DOC unravels a long piece of
string and holds it up.)*

DOC. *(Fanatically)* See this? This is one way I can get a
duck. And I figure it all out by myself.

SWEENEY. *(Laughing)* He's going to lasso a duck.

DOC. That's it! That's it! See, when I'm a kid out West I
catch gophers with a piece of string. I make a little lasso and
put it over their holes and I wait . . . and I wait . . . and
I wait. Then when they stick their heads up to look around,
I quick pull the lasso—and I got a gopher.

OSCAR. But ducks ain't gophers.

DOC. I know it, I know it. So I got the same thing figured out
—but for ducks. See this piece of string—see them little
bumps—that's pieces of lead. See them other bumps, that's
bottlecorks. I go down by the lake, see, and I make a lasso
out of this. Then I put it in the water. The lead pulls the
lasso down under the water so's the ducks don't see it, and
the bottlecorks hold it up offen the bottom. Then I just wait,

and wait, and wait—until a duck swims over it and I yank quick and I got a duck.

SWEENEY. What you going to do, send the ducks invitations to swim over? (DOC *looks at others anxiously, then, as* SWEENEY *contemptuously waves his hand, he continues quickly, frantically.)*

DOC. But that's only one way. Here's something better. *(Grabs another long piece of string with something tied on the end, and holds it up)* See this? It's a potato. Ducks like 'em. I float the potato on the water and pretty soon a duck comes along and gobbles it up. But then he can't let go, and I just pull in quick with the string . . .

STEVE. *(With less rage)* Like he pulls in the eels.

DOC. If that don't work, this will. *(Almost crying)* I can't be wrong all the time. *(Shoves hand in pocket and holds it out; then quietly, persuasively)* You know what this is, fellas? It's corn. I been saving it for weeks. And I got enough to get a duck. See, we make a little path from the lake up to some bushes. Ducks like corn better'n anything, so they gotta follow it; and when the duck gets up to the bushes . . . (DOC *suddenly clutches hands together in the act of wringing a duck's neck)* You got to believe me, fellas—I know I can get one of them ducks.

OLD MAN NELSON. *(To* OSCAR) What do you think, friend?

OSCAR. I dunno nothing about getting ducks; but if you get one I'll cook it.

DOC. There you are, fellas, that settles it, don't it? I can get the duck and he can cook it.

OLD MAN NELSON. Ducks ain't easy to cook, even after you get 'em.

OSCAR. *(With pride)* I can cook a duck blindfolded and one arm tied behind me. I'm a short-order cook by profession.

OLD MAN NELSON. What do you know about that, boys. We got a real short-order cook with us.

SWEENEY. *(With sweet sarcasm)* I didn't know ducks was a short-order.

OSCAR. I ain't always a short-order cook, for Christ sake.

OLD MAN NELSON. Hey, what if he can get a duck.

STEVE. *(Calmed down now)* All right; I warned youse; I warned youse.

OLD MAN NELSON. Are you sure you can get a duck?

DOC. *(Crossing himself)* I never been so sure of anything in my life.

OLD MAN NELSON. By golly, maybe he can get a duck.

DOC. *(Grabbing* OSCAR*)* You agree with me too, don't you?

STEVE. *(Wavering a little—to* OLD MAN NELSON*)* You don't think he can get a duck, do you?

OLD MAN NELSON. Yes, I think maybe he can.

CHARLIE. How de hell's he going to get a duck with dat crap?

STEVE. He's crazy, I tell you.

OLD MAN NELSON. *(Excitedly)* Here, boys—I got the way to settle it. We'll vote on it. Who wants a duck?

DOC. Fellas, I can get one of them ducks..

SWEENEY. Quack—diddy-quack-quack—quack-quack.

OSCAR. I'll cook it. (CHARLIE *makes an ugly sound.)*

OLD MAN NELSON. *(Jumping around)* The ayes got it, and we're going to get a duck. We're going to get a duck. A nice, big, fat, juicy duck.

OSCAR. I want a leg.

DOC. I want a leg, too.

OLD MAN NELSON. Give me the other one.

SWEENEY. Now they're going to get a duck with three legs.

OLD MAN NELSON. Here, I got a way to divide this duck that'll end this jawing in jigtime. *(Pulls a twig off a bush, breaks it up, and turns to others)* Now the ones with the longest sticks get their pick. (DOC *and* OSCAR *study and deliberate before picking their sticks.* SWEENEY, CHARLIE, STEVE *and* WILER, *who is still stretched out on bench, take no part.* DOC *and* OSCAR *pick their sticks, then* OLD MAN NELSON *goes over to* SWEENEY *and* CHARLIE.*)*

OLD MAN NELSON. Come on, boys, pick a stick. It can't do no harm.

SWEENEY. Save mine for later. You'll need it to pick the duck out of your teeth.

CHARLIE. *(Waving his hand at* OLD MAN NELSON*)* Gwan, yuh old billy-goat, yuh're batty. (JOE, *a youth of 15 or 16, carrying a bundle, enters* R. *and timidly stops just inside entrance.* OLD MAN NELSON *sees him and hustles over with sticks.)*

OSCAR. *(To* DOC, *who is straightening out lasso)* Did you ever catch a duck with that?

DOC. Not yet, but we can't miss. I can't go to sleep last night thinking about it. I don't know why I never figure it out before.

OLD MAN NELSON. *(To* JOE) You're just in time, sonny—pick a stick. . . . It's for a duck.

SWEENEY. *(As* JOE *seems puzzled)* They're keeping it cool in the lake so it don't go bad.

OLD MAN NELSON. Pay him no mind, sonny, just take a stick. . . . You picked a good one, too. *(Looks around, sees* STEVE, *walks over to him and wordlessly holds out sticks)* Go ahead, take one. Things is going to be different this time.

STEVE. Leave me alone.

OLD MAN NELSON. Honest, I can feel it in my bones; we're going to get a duck.

STEVE. For Christ sake, leave me alone, will you?

OLD MAN NELSON. *(Lowering his voice)* Here, I'll pick one for you. (STEVE *looks up at* OLD MAN NELSON, *as latter pulls a stick, then turns his head away.)*

OLD MAN NELSON. We're all set now, boys. Let's measure 'em. *(Simultaneously they all hold their sticks out.)*

OSCAR. I got the longest. I take a leg.

OLD MAN NELSON. *(To* STEVE) And you got the other leg.

DOC. Save me some of the breast.

OLD MAN NELSON. It's my turn now, and I like a wing. *(To* JOE) You're next, sonny. *(Lowering his voice)* Take the other wing.

JOE. Sure, anything.

SWEENEY. I'll take the wishbone.

CHARLIE. Kin I pull it wid yuh?

OLD MAN NELSON. *(Indicating* SWEENEY *and* CHARLIE) Give them the side and back and the duck's all divided.

JOE. *(Pointing to* WILER *on bench)* How about him?

OSCAR. He gets the gizzard.

OLD MAN NELSON. Now, boys, let's get the duck! Let's get the duck.

OSCAR. *(As* DOC *starts off* R.) Wait a minute, till I get everybody's order straight.

OLD MAN NELSON. We can do that when we get the duck, boy.

OSCAR. I'm doing it now so's to save arguments later. *(Surveying his clientele)* A leg for me . . . a leg for you . . . a wing for you . . . a wing for you . . . the breast for you

. . . the sides and back for them . . . and the gizzard for him. That's got it, ain't it?

SWEENEY. No, I'm having the Blueplate Special.

OSCAR. Go to hell.

DOC. Hey, Steve, will you give me a hand?

OLD MAN NELSON. *(Gently shoving* STEVE *over toward* DOC*)* You two go together and one can watch while the other yanks. Time's a-wasting, let's get going.

STEVE. I ain't going with him if we never get a duck.

DOC. I can't be wrong all the time, Steve.

OLD MAN NELSON. I feel it in my bones, you're going to get a duck. (DOC *hurries off. Meanwhile,* OSCAR *and* JOE *have been hustling around gathering up sticks and branches for the fire. They arrange them in a pile near bench.)*

OSCAR. This ain't going to be bad at all. Now who's got a knife? (JOE *yanks out jack-knife and hands it to* OSCAR.) Okay, it's got a good edge. Now, we need a bag or some papers for the feathers and the guts. (OLD MAN NELSON *quickly unbuttons his coat, pulls out a newspaper and hands it to* OSCAR.)

OLD MAN NELSON. Is that enough?

OSCAR. *(Surveying the layout with satisfaction)* Everything's copesetic. Now bring on the ducks. Then come and get it.

OLD MAN NELSON. How you going to cook 'em?

OSCAR. *(Pondering)* I think I'd better bake them.

OLD MAN NELSON. *(Chuckling)* Oh, there's nothing better than baked duck. *(Then, to* JOE*)* Do you like ducks, sonny?

JOE. *(Grinning)* I like anything.

OLD MAN NELSON. You got to go some to beat duck, don't you? Where do you come from?

JOE. Vermont.

OLD MAN NELSON. That's one place I never been.

JOE. It's the only place I've ever been—until yesterday.

OLD MAN NELSON. Have you got good ducks up there?

JOE. Yeah, we got pretty good ones.

OLD MAN NELSON. *(Getting up and walking around, excitedly)* Everything works out for the best sometimes, don't it? I would of been sleeping in the mission tonight . . . if I was on time. *(Chuckling)* But if I was sleeping in the mission I wouldn't be getting any duck, would I?

CHARLIE. Dat's where yuh belong, yuh old fogey, in a mission.

SWEENEY. I bet he's a hymn-singer, too.

OLD MAN NELSON. Sure I sing the hymns. I like to sing 'em. And I know 'em all by heart. Don't you like hymns?

SWEENEY. Yeah, like I like a dose of poison.

OLD MAN NELSON. I know one you like; everybody likes that one; I ain't seen nobody yet don't like it. It's the best of them all. *(He starts right in singing it)*

'There's not a friend like the low'ly Jesus
No not one, No not one
Jesus knows all about our struggles
He will guide till the day is done
There's not a friend like the low'ly Jesus
No not one, No not one.'

(SWEENEY gets up solemnly, takes off his derby, holds it in front of him like a drum and starts beating it with his fist as, he marches around summer-house.)

SWEENEY. *(Marching)* D-boom da-boom . . . da-boom-boom-boom . . . da-boom da-boom . . . da-boom-boom-boom. *(He comes to a halt in middle of stage and continues rhythmically beating the derby as he testifies)* 'Brothers and Sisters: I was nothing but a bum when the Salvation Army takes me to its bosom; I don't have a coat on my back, and my behind is sticking out. But they give me clothes for my body, and food for my belly, and tonight, I'm so happy, I could beat the living bejesus outa this goddam drum.' *(As he delivers the above he accompanies it with a terrific bastinado on the derby. CHARLIE jumps up and shoots his arms out spread-eagle fashion.)*

CHARLIE. Hallelujah! *(SWEENEY and CHARLIE burst into laughter.)*

OLD MAN NELSON. *(With his hands over his ears)* I won't listen to that! I won't listen to it!

CHARLIE. *(Dropping down on bench)* I'll split anudder gut.

OLD MAN NELSON. *(Pointing an admonitory finger at them)* And you'll never get a duck, talking like that.

SWEENEY. By the time you get a duck, this'll be called Hungry Pop Park.

CHARLIE. *(Suddenly belligerent)* Fer Christ's sake, I'll bet yuh was never even in Madison Square in de old days.

JOE. *(Who has been looking off R.)* Hey, here comes somebody running.

OSCAR. *(Running to his side)* Where?

JOE. *(Pointing)* There, see him?

OSCAR. I see him now. I see him. It's the little guy. (STEVE, *who has stretched out on bench, sits up.)*

JOE. Look at him come.

OSCAR. *(Wonderstruck)* And he's got a duck. (STEVE *gets quickly to his feet and joins others.)*

OLD MAN NELSON. I knowed it; I knowed it. Don't I say he'd get one. *(A duck is heard quacking.)*

OSCAR. Listen to that.

JOE. It's a big one too; I can see it.

OLD MAN NELSON. *(To OSCAR)* How long does it take to cook a duck?

SWEENEY. *(To CHARLIE)* I think they got one. *(A crash off-stage.)*

OSCAR. *(Shouting)* Look out.

OLD MAN NELSON. What happened?

JOE. He tripped.

OSCAR. Goddam.

JOE. I don't see him now. *(Scuffling, mutterings and a duck quacking angrily are heard offstage.)*

OLD MAN NELSON. I don't see that far; what's going on?

DOC. *(Offstage)* Come back here.

JOE. I see 'em now. The duck's getting away.

STEVE. *(Shouting)* Don't let it back in the lake. Head it off! Head it off, Doc!

OLD MAN NELSON. I wish I could see what was going on.

JOE. *(Running off)* I'll head it off.

OSCAR. There they go, and he's gaining on it.

OLD MAN NELSON. I hope the duck trips.

OSCAR. I don't see 'em now.

JOE. *(Offstage)* Head him off the other way.

OSCAR. *(Pointing)* They went behind that bush.

OLD MAN NELSON. Are they out of the bushes yet? (OSCAR *shakes his head.)*

CHARLIE. *(To SWEENEY)* An' yuh t'ink dey got one.

OLD MAN NELSON. Do you see 'em yet?

OSCAR. Uh uh. And I don't hear nothing. It's back in the lake by this time.

OLD MAN NELSON. Don't give up; he'll get another one. (DOC *appears from* L. *His clothes are torn, his shoes muddy, and two or three duck feathers cling to his overcoat. He walks despondently to* C. *of summer-house, stops and absent-mindedly picks off duck feathers. He can hardly get his breath. Others all look at him, but no one speaks.)*

DOC. *(Painfully)* I had it . . . right in my . . . hands . . .

OLD MAN NELSON. *(Sympathetically)* You tripped, didn't you? (DOC *nods.)*

OSCAR. *(Dully)* Why didn't you wring its neck?

DOC. I was just thinking the same thing myself. (JOE *reappears.)*

OLD MAN NELSON. *(To* JOE) Was it a big one?

JOE. Yeah.

DOC. I just got a jinx on me, that's all. I'm a Jonah. (DOC *cries and others look at him curiously)* I'm just a goddam Jonah.

OLD MAN NELSON. *(Patting him on back)* Don't talk like that, boy. You said you was going to get a duck, and you got a duck, didn't you? Accidents happen to anybody. *(Ducks are heard quacking again.)* There's lots more where that one come from. Hear 'em? You ain't no Jonah and you can get a duck; I know you can.

SWEENEY. Quack—diddy-quack-quack . . .

OLD MAN NELSON. *(Indignantly)* You leave him alone, you no-good.

SWEENEY. *(Finishing up quickly)* . . . Quack-quack.

OLD MAN NELSON. *(To* DOC) Don't you get down in the dumps. Everybody's counting on you. (DOC *looks at* OLD MAN NELSON *for a moment as latter keeps nodding his head encouragingly. Then he quickly turns to bench and starts searching around.)*

DOC. *(His optimism coming back)* Where is it? Who took it? I'll get one this time. Where is the corn?

STEVE. Here it is. *(He scoops it up from bench and holds it out to* DOC.)

OLD MAN NELSON. *(Who has been watching* STEVE) Why don't you give him a hand? *(He pats* STEVE *on back and nods his head.)*

DOC. If you work with me this time, Steve, we just can't miss. There's ducks all over that lake.

OLD MAN NELSON. Go ahead, boy, two heads is always better than one.

DOC. *(Excited again)* You keep the corn, Steve, and I'll take the lasso.

STEVE. I'm not waiting in no bushes for ducks like I wait for the squirrels. *(Wordlessly* DOC *hands* STEVE *lasso.* STEVE *hesitates a moment, then takes it.)*

OLD MAN NELSON. Now let's get going, let's get going.

DOC. You work one side of the lake, Steve, and I'll work the other, but we gotta figure out a signal so's we'll know who gets the first duck.

SWEENEY. *(Suddenly jumping up)* I got the signal for you— I just figure it out; listen to this. *(Imitating Donald Duck)* 'Oh, boy; oh, boy; I got a little duckie, and he's headed for the pottie.' *(Ducks in the lake send up a clamorous response.)*

OSCAR. Hey, will you shut up. You want to tip off all the ducks in the lake?

SWEENEY. *(Snickering to* CHARLIE*)* I don't know my own strength.

DOC. Here, I got it! Soon as one of us gets a duck, whistle once, an' two if he don't.

OLD MAN NELSON. Right; one if you get it, two if you don't. Now on your way, boys. *(*STEVE *goes off to R.)*

OSCAR. *(To* DOC, *who is hurrying after him)* Look out where you're going this time, buddy, and don't trip again. *(*DOC *stops at entrance and turns.)*

DOC. I'm going to get us some grub this time, fellas. I can't stand it no longer.

OLD MAN NELSON. You can do it, boy. Go to it, and God bless you. *(*DOC *leaves.* OLD MAN NELSON *picks up one of the duck feathers.)* Before I'm just hungry; now I'm hungry for duck. *(Ducks are heard again; then a voice calling.)*

VOICE. *(Offstage)* Here, duck . . . here, duck . . . here, duck.

OLD MAN NELSON. *(Looking off)* What are they doing that for?

SWEENEY. They're coaxing the ducks into the bushes so they can sprinkle a little salt on their tails.

OSCAR. I hear of hog-calling. *(Shaking his head)* But duck-calling is something new. *(A lion roars.)*

OLD MAN NELSON. They ain't fooling around with them lions, are they?

OSCAR. I give up. But if they get a lion I'll cook it.

SWEENEY. I want a leg.

OLD MAN NELSON. *(Chuckling)* That's a good one. (CHARLIE, *who has remained aloof during the discussion of the duck, gets up and walks over toward others.)*

CHARLIE. No wonder yuh guys is bums. An' yuh'll always be bums. And yuh wanna know why? 'cause yuh don't use de old noggin. Dere's six of youse an' yuh're only gointa glom one duck, fer Christ sake. *(Laughs—then stops and becomes belligerent)* Why, I kin get two ducks meself; what de hell yuh t'ink of dat?

OSCAR. Well, nobody's stopping you.

CHARLIE. What yuh doin', calling me a liar?

OLD MAN NELSON. No, he just means if you can get two ducks, go get 'em; and he'll cook 'em for us.

CHARLIE. Oh, yuh don't t'ink I kin get 'em eider, yuh old fogey.

OLD MAN NELSON. Sure, I think you can get 'em.

CHARLIE. I'm gointa show yuh lousy bastards somet'ing. Me, all by me lonesome. I'm gointa git two ducks wid o'ny dis *(Pointing to his head)*, de old noggin, an' dese *(He holds up his fists)*, an' widout no goddam strings er potatoes er corn. Jist watch me. *(He straightens his shoulders and lunges out to L. as though bell had just rung for the first round.)*

OLD MAN NELSON. I bet he gets 'em, too.

SWEENEY. If his foot don't slip again. *(A single shrill whistle offstage, followed by a lot of quack-quacking.)*

OSCAR. There goes the signal.

OLD MAN NELSON. *(To JOE)* Do you see anything?

JOE. Not yet.

OLD MAN NELSON. Keep a sharp eye, lad, and let me know as soon as you do. *(Ducks are again heard, followed by two sharp whistles.)*

OSCAR. What the hell does that mean?

OLD MAN NELSON. Maybe it means they got one duck but they ain't got the other one yet.

OSCAR. You're nuts. (STEVE *enters, carrying a* MAN. *He is*

OLD MAN NELSON. *(Excited)* Maybe it's a deer.

JOE. Here comes one of 'em, and he's got something big.

well dressed but his clothes are wet and muddy. STEVE *puts him down on floor.)*

OLD MAN NELSON. Is he dead?

STEVE. Yeah; dead-drunk.

OSCAR. Was that him we hear yelling?

STEVE. *(Nodding)* I almost got a duck, a good one. *(Pointing to* MAN*)* Then he's gotta butt in and fall in the lake.

OLD MAN NELSON. You sure he ain't dead?

STEVE. No, he just swalleys some lake water.

JOE. I know what to do. *(*JOE *quickly straddles* MAN *and starts pumping his arms.)*

STEVE. We'll never get a duck now. He drove 'em all to the middle of the lake. *(*MAN *rolls his head around and* JOE *gets off his chest. Slowly* MAN *sits up and blinks his eyes.)*

MAN. What happened?

OLD MAN NELSON. You all right?

MAN. *(Feeling his clothes)* How did I get wet?

STEVE. You was in the lake.

MAN. What was I doing in the lake?

STEVE. You fell in.

MAN. Oh, my God! I'm sick! Oh, I'm going to die! Jesus Christ! Oh, oh, oh! *(He gets unsteadily to his feet and they help him over to bench.)* I've never been this sick; Oh, Jesus, will somebody give me a drink? Please, just one drink and I'll be all right. *(Suddenly* MAN *starts crying.)*

STEVE. What are you blubbering about?

MAN. I'm a no-good bastard, that's what I am, a no-good bastard. Where did she go?

OSCAR. Where did who go?

MAN. My wife.

STEVE. We ain't seen your wife.

MAN. *(Crying again)* After all I've done for her, after all we've been through, she left me. *(Slapping his chest)* I'm wet through to the skin. I've got to get out of these clothes before I catch my death. Christ, I'm sick. I wish I were dead. Can't you give me just *one* drink?

OSCAR. How about you giving him something for fishing you out of the lake.

MAN. *(Rummaging in his pockets)* She's got my money. She's got everything. Now she's left me. *(Cries again)* Oh,

God, I'm cold. *(Becoming belligerent)* Who pushed me in the lake?

STEVE. Nobody pushed you. You fell in.

MAN. Oh, you think I'm drunk, too. She thinks I'm drunk. I drink too much, do I? I ought to know whether I drink too much. *(Crying again)* I haven't a friend in the world.

OSCAR. You should of left him in the lake.

MAN. Oh, I've got to have a drink. I'm just a no-good bastard, that's what I am. Getting myself all wet like this. *(Staggers toward entrance, then stops and turns)* Where's my hat?

STEVE. How the hell do we know.

MAN. You'll never see me in this condition again. I'm through. Just one more drink, then I'm through. Done. Never again . . . *(Crying again)* Somebody pushed me in the lake. *(Staggers off.)*

SWEENEY. *(Snickering)* Did you get a whiff of his breath? It smelled just like the good old days.

OLD MAN NELSON. *(Shaking his head)* Everybody's got their troubles. Did you see him cry?

OSCAR. Now, there's a guy with good clothes, a home and a job, and he's drinking himself to death over some broad. I never see the broad yet that could do that to me.

SWEENEY. They're all whores.

OLD MAN NELSON. *(Indignant)* Don't you say that.

SWEENEY. Hey, I wonder why they ain't got any whorehouses in this town?

OSCAR. *(Shaking his head)* He can't fill his gut and he's worrying about broads.

SWEENEY. Food ain't everything.

OSCAR. Yeah? Well, I like to put a bowl of soup down and put a broad next to it and see which you take.

SWEENEY. The bowl of soup.

OSCAR. You're damn right.

SWEENEY. Yeah. Then I'm strong for the broad. Then another bowl of soup . . . then the broad. Make it vegetable.

MAN. *(Offstage)* Here, duck; here, duck; here, duck.

STEVE. If he falls in the lake again he can stay there. (CHARLIE *enters from* L., *muttering to himself. He looks around the bench searching for someone.)*

CHARLIE. Where's dat little punk? Come on, where's he at?

OLD MAN NELSON. *(Without enthusiasm)* He's still after the ducks.

CHARLIE. I'll give him de ducks. I'm gointa fix de son of a bitch wid his ducks. *(He makes a couple of practice swings, then grabs* STEVE, *who is sitting down on bench, and yanks him up)* Git outa me way, punk. *(Sits down and continues half to himself)* Nobody's gointa make a goddam fool outa me. *(He punches down between his legs)* Yuh'd t'ink I was back in de ring, fer Christ sake. I jab at de bastards, an' dey duck quicker'n I kin duck. Where is he? I got me goddam feet wet. *(Raising his voice)* Do yuh hear me talking to yuh, yuh lousy bastards? Where's de little punk?

OLD MAN NELSON. He's still out after a duck.

CHARLIE. *(Swinging his fists again)* He betta git a duck.

OSCAR. *(To* JOE) I guess it just ain't our night for ducks. *(*JOE *looks at sticks but makes no move. They are all silent now, waiting; no one wants to give up. A trolley-car is heard rumbling over the tracks.* SWEENEY, *who is at* R., *becomes alert as he stares off.)*

SWEENEY. Here comes the little guy. *(Everyone looks toward* SWEENEY, *but no one moves.)*

SWEENEY. He's coming very careful. *(Excitement shows in his voice)* He's got something. He's got it wrapped up in his coat. (OSCAR *stands up.* OLD MAN NELSON *clasps his hands together and rocks back and forth. One by one all stand up, even* WILER.)

SWEENEY. Here he comes. And he's got it! By God, he's got it!

OSCAR. *(Grinning)* Give me elbow room. (DOC *enters from* R. *carrying something wrapped up in his overcoat. His face is scratched and his clothes are torn in several places.)*

DOC. *(Breathlessly)* I got it, Steve. I got it. *(This is the signal they have been waiting for and they all come to life. They slap one another on the back. They grin and jump about like children.)*

OLD MAN NELSON. Hurray for the little guy. I knowed he'd do it.

SWEENEY. *(To* STEVE) I don't say nothing before, but my gut was killing me.

STEVE. So was mine. (CHARLIE *just stands and grins at* DOC.)

OSCAR. Out of my way, boys. Give it to me, buddy. Give me

that duck. (DOC *puts overcoat down on ground; kneels beside it.*)

DOC. I couldn't get a duck. They was too fast for me. But I got something *(Hesitates)* I think is going to be just as good.

OLD MAN NELSON. Let's have it, boy, let's have it! (DOC *looks up at them all for a moment, then slowly opens overcoat and reveals a small monkey.*)

OLD MAN NELSON. *(Stunned)* It's a monkey.

CHARLIE. *(Kneeling down beside* DOC) Yeah. Sure. An' I bet he's gointa be good. Look at dem legs.

DOC. *(Looking questioningly at the others)* I had a hard time getting it.

CHARLIE. *(Slapping* DOC *on back)* Yuh're a right gie, Willie. *(All stand dumbfounded, looking at the monkey)* Look, he's trying to bite me. *(Chuckling)* I'm gointa be biting him in a minute.

SWEENEY. I got an uncle uset to look just like that . . . Jesus . . . *(He laughs, but is half hysterical.)*

OLD MAN NELSON. I won't eat that.

CHARLIE. *(Becoming belligerent)* What de hell's de matter wid it? Fer Christ sake, yuh lousy bastards git good grub den yuh don't want it.

OSCAR. What do you think we are—cannibals?

CHARLIE. Ta hell wid 'em. Yuh an' me'll split it between us, Willie.

DOC. It was the only thing I could get. (STEVE *turns his back and goes over to bench.*)

CHARLIE. An' yuh couldn't do better. *(Patting* DOC *on back again)* Yuh're a right gie, Willie. *(While* CHARLIE's *head is turned,* OSCAR *stoops down, picks up monkey and walks over to entrance on* L. CHARLIE *sees him just as he lets monkey go. He gets to his feet)* What de hell yuh doing, yuh lousy bastard? *(He rushes over to* OSCAR, *grabs him, and throws him halfway across summer-house, then looks frantically around for monkey. When he doesn't see it he turns toward others)* All right, yuh asked fer it, yuh dirty son of a bitch. Nobody's gointa steal me grub and get away wit it. Come on, I'm gointa give it to yuh. I'm gointa take on every one of youse. *(Whips off his coat and throws it on ground)* I'm gointa kill yuh. I'm gointa kill yuh.

WILER. *(Runs over to* CHARLIE, *screaming)* Give it to 'em.

They don't let me sleep. Give it to 'em. Give it to 'em. Give it to 'em. (CHARLIE *turns on* WILER *and knocks him down.*)

OLD MAN NELSON. Don't; don't; ain't we got enough agin us without being agin one another.

CHARLIE. Dat's one. Now, come on. Come on an' git your lumps. (*He moves from one side to other with his fists up. The men move instinctively away from him each time.*) Yuh ain't gointa take grub away from me and git away wid it. Yuh fooled wid de wrong punk dis time. I fight some of de best of 'em, seester? Come on, yuh dirty muzzlers. Ever hear what I done to Danny McGovern? Yeah; I'm de gie Charlie Turner—dat's me. Come on. I'm gointa give yuh what I give dat yellow bastard. (*He is near one of the logs supporting roof, and he punches it with all his force*) Dat's what I done ta him, wid me bare knuckles too. In Joisey City. He's got me going de foist five round but den I git him where I want him. I got yuh where I want yuh now. (CHARLIE *is now in front of log. He stands there a moment swaying from side to side*) Let's see if yuh kin take it. (*Suddenly he starts hitting log as hard as he can with both hands, and every time his knuckles beat against the wood the others wince*) How do yuh like dat? (*Blow*) And dat? (*Blow*) And dat? (*Blow; he laughs a little*) Yuh son of a bitch. (*Blow . . . blow . . . blow.*)

SWEENEY. (*Shrilly*) Why don't somebody stop him?

OSCAR. (*Who has moved over near* CHARLIE) Hey, old timer, let's see you do that trick you was doing with the handkerchief. (CHARLIE *turns menacingly on* OSCAR.)

CHARLIE. (*Crouching*) Yuh can't take it, kin yuh? See how yuh like dis?

OSCAR. (*Steadily*) That trick you was doing with the handkerchief, when you was ducking.

CHARLIE. (*Blinking*) Huh?

OSCAR. You know, on the handkerchief. (*Mechanically* CHARLIE *pulls handkerchief out of his pocket, puts it on ground and stands on it.*)

CHARLIE. Go ahead; jab me. (OSCAR *purposely jabs wide of* CHARLIE'S *head.*)

OSCAR. (*After several misses*) I can't hit you.

CHARLIE. An' I don't move offen dis noserag. (*Stands, his arms hanging limp and blinks at* OSCAR.)

DOC. *(Who is still kneeling beside his overcoat, looking at* STEVE, *gets up)* Steve. (STEVE *stretches out on bench and turns his back.* DOC *looks around at others, and then picks up his overcoat, slowly walks over to bench and stretches out.)*

CHARLIE. Jist try and hit me.

OSCAR. I couldn't hit you if I got four arms. *(Then looking at* CHARLIE'S *hands)* You better go down to the lake and wash them cuts.

CHARLIE. Dey don't bother me none. *(The fight is all out of him now. He is just a tired old man as he ambles over to bench and stretches out. Hope is gone now and they all stretch out on bench with the exception of* OLD MAN NELSON *and* JOE.*)*

OLD MAN NELSON. You better go to sleep, sonny.

JOE. I'm kind of 'fraid.

OLD MAN NELSON. I know. I know. I been afraid manys the time. Afraid of more things than I remember. And I been afraid of nothing at all but just the dark. Many's the time. But everybody's afraid in the night. *(Then with just the trace of a chuckle)* So you got lots of company, and it don't matter so much. *(Pats his knee)* Here, sonny, put your head down here. (JOE *looks at him for a moment, then puts his head down.)* That's it. Now, say a little prayer; it always helps. Say a little prayer; I never knowed it to fail. *(Patting boy's shoulder and singing very softly)* 'There's not a friend like the low'ly Jesus— No not one— No not one . : .' *(His voice fades away and his head falls forward on his chest. After a pause, harsh yapping barks of seals are heard.)*

OSCAR. *(Raising his head a little)* They're giving the seals their breakfast.

WILER. *(Also raising his head)* Yeah, it must be about the time. *(They are all quiet now. From far off comes the sound of a boat whistle, followed by: the clop-clop of a horse; a solitary automobile harn; a trolley-car bumping along the tracks; and, finally, far away and very faint, the quack-quack of the ducks.)*

END OF PLAY

HOME LIFE
OF A BUFFALO

CHARACTERS

Josey Quinn
Eddie Quinn
Joe Quinn, *their son*
Molly Shaeffer
Otto Shaeffer

A light house-keeping apartment in a theatrical room-ing house in the West Forties off Broadway. Actually it is a large furnished room rather than an apartment, with a door U.R. leading to a hallway and a window in C. of wall L. opening on a fire escape, part of which can be seen. Theatrical pictures are tacked up on all the walls and next to window on the R. is a poster on which this legend is prominently displayed: "THE THREE DANCING QUINNS." Against upper wall C. is an old-fashioned folding bed with a full length mirror on its front. To L. of the bed is a combination bureau-wardrobe. Downstage from window a folding screen masks an ice-box and small gas stove. Against wall on R. is a small cot. To R. of door is a speaking tube. A large table in C. of the room and several chairs, placed here and there.

JOE QUINN. *a small boy of 9, is in front of the folding bed facing the mirror. He wears a flashy suit topped by an Eton collar, and his hair is cut in Buster Brown style. He is wearing a small top hat. He removes latter with a flourish and takes an elaborate bow. He 'exits' from in front of mirror, then reappears immediately and takes another bow to mirror. As he is doing this a key from the door is heard and he jerks out of the bow, looks apprehensively at door, then scurries to table and hides under it.*

JOSEY QUINN, *a nice-looking woman in her middle*

*forties, enters. She carries a small bundle of groceries
which she places on table. She removes her hat and coat,
sits down and relaxes.*
JOE *sticks his head cautiously out from under table and
looks around.*
JOSEY *sees him and stifles a scream.*

JOE. It's only me, Mom.

JOSEY. You almost scared the daylights out of me— How
did you get in here?

JOE. By the fire escape.

JOSEY. Didn't I tell you not to come in the fire escape?

JOE. I know you did, Mom—but Mrs. Fuller was standin'
down by the front door.

JOSEY. What if she was, Joey— You don't have to be afraid
of her. *(She takes groceries from table and crossing to ice
box begins putting things away during ensuing scene.)*

JOE. She don't like me.

JOSEY. That's just your imagination . . . Now, tell me, what
have you been doin' with yourself all afternoon?

JOE. Oh, learnin' some new steps Pop showed me an' practicin' a few bows.

JOSEY. Why didn't you do some studyin'? . . . Your report
card came today an' it's worse than ever.

JOE. *(Going into dance routine)* I guess I'm just no good at
school.

JOSEY. You don't *try* to be any good at it, Joe.

JOE. *(Executing a difficult step)* There's just some things I
can't get—like fractions . . . I missed 'em . . . we was on
the road that year—'member?

JOSEY. I know that, Joey—but you're bright an' you can
catch up if you study hard.

JOE. All right, Mom—I'll try.

JOSEY. Maybe school don't seem important to you now—but
if you've got an education nothin' can stop you . . . You
can go any place . . . Just take Abraham Lincoln—he didn't
have nothin' but he studied hard—an' wouldn't give up—an'
look where he got.

JOE. *(Stopping dance)* I want to show you something, Mom.
(Does an exceedingly difficult step) Do you think Abraham
Lincoln coulda done that when he was my age?

JOSEY. Forget the *act*— There's lots more important things in life . . .

JOE. Gee, what if Pop heard you say that . . .

JOSEY. Why can't you see what Mama means . . . She wants you to *be* something . . .

JOE. Well, I'm gonna be a great hoofer—just like Pop . . . That's what you want me to be, don't you? . . . *(Then as she doesn't answer)* Don't you, Mom?

JOSEY. *(After hesitating)* Oh, of course I do, Joey . . . But I also want you to study hard just in case you ever want to be something else.

JOE. I'll never want to be anything else—but just to satisfy you, Mom, I'll try to study a little harder.

JOSEY. That's the way I like to hear you talk. (JOE *sits down, opens book, as* JOSEY *begins preparing supper.)*

JOE. Momma . . . I was just thinkin'—if I'm awful quiet can I take it easy till supper—then I'll *really* study.

JOSEY. All right—but after supper, an' that's a promise. (JOE *folds his arms and is quiet for a second, then jumps up and stands on his head.)*

JOSEY. Is that your idea of bein' quiet?

JOE. I'm quiet, Mom—I thought while I was doin' nothing I'd practice my head-stand. (EDDIE QUINN, *a man of fifty, appears on fire escape outside window. He is charged with energy and full of enthusiasm. Under one arm he carries a package. He hops into the room.)*

JOSEY. Why can't you come in the right way for a change? You got him doin' it.

EDDIE. It's quicker that way.

JOE. *(Tumbling out of the head-stand)* Hello, Pop, I missed you.

EDDIE. Did you get that routine I showed you?

JOE. Sure I got it, what do think I am, a dummy?

EDDIE. Josey, our troubles is over—startin' the last half of next week.

JOSEY. What did you line up—another roadhouse?

EDDIE. We're gonna play a real honest-to-God theater— again . . . An' we're gonna keep on playin' 'em.

JOE. Wow!

JOSEY. You mean you got the last half of the week?

EDDIE. The last half—the first half—an' more time to follow than you can count. *(He whirls* JOSEY *around.)*

JOE. Oh, boy— Oh, boy— Oh, boy.

EDDIE. Don't I always tell you, Josey—if you fight for a thing long enough an' hard enough—it's just gotta come true.

JOSEY. I can't believe it . . . Sounds too good to be true . . . We'll be able to look the butcher in the eye again.

EDDIE. That's all behind us . . . We're gonna wipe the slate clean.

JOE. It's a good thing I got that routine, ain't it, Pop?

EDDIE. Yes, sir, Joey—'cause we're gonna need it . . .

JOSEY. *(Calming down)* Just a minute, Ed . . .

EDDIE. Up— Up— I know what you're gonna say, Baby— "Are they bringin' vaudeville back—or takin' us on another goosechase?"

JOSEY. Well, are they?

EDDIE. Not this time—because I made 'em put it down in black-an'-white— *(He holds up contract)* There's our Declaration of Independence . . . Vaudeville ain't comin' back . . . Vaudeville *is* back. *(Spontaneously he and* JOE *do a joyful dance step.)*

JOSEY. My God, you really got a *contract!*

EDDIE. Signed, sealed and delivered . . .

JOSEY. I thought they stopped makin' 'em . . . Eddie, it's *wonderful!* . . . *(She whirls him around.)*

EDDIE. That's enough celebratin' . . . Now we gotta go into action . . . *(He pauses for effect)* Josey, I'm gonna revolutionize the act.

JOSEY. Now hadn't you just better leave well enough alone?

EDDIE. That's what wrong with our profession . . . It don't keep up with the times . . . It don't look ahead . . . It just makes me sick to see all the guys with real genuine talent losin' faith, lettin' their acts slip, gettin' outta practice . . . Where do you think they're gonna be with vaudeville comin' back—they're gonna be lookin' out the window. *(Fervently)* But, by God, I wont be.

JOSEY. Look, Ed, I'm for every improvement we can make.

EDDIE. All right, do you ever stop to think why our crossfire don't get big belly laughs any more?

JOSEY. It's kinda hard to tell,—we been playin' Elks Clubs, smokers an' roadhouses so long.

EDDIE. That's no alibi . . . The reason is the way we're lead-in' into it . . . Why, every ham-fat double in the business comes on wavin' an' bumps.

JOSEY. But we gotta work into the gags some way.

EDDIE. Sure, but there's no law against originality, is there? . . . Hand me that package, Joe.

JOE. Okay, Pop. (EDDIE *starts taking off his shoes.*)

EDDIE. I got a way of freshenin' that routine up that's dyna-mite

JOE. *(Handing him package)* What is it, Pop?

EDDIE. Them buzzards in radio an' the talkies never miss a trick—an' from now on *we* ain't gonna miss any.

JOSEY. Now don't start worryin' about them again.

EDDIE. You gotta worry about 'em . . . They lay awake nights figurin' new gags to take the bread outa cur mouths . . . Take radio—they know the public is clamorin' for vaude-ville—so what do they do?

JOE. What, Pop?

EDDIE. Why, they lure the public into the studios so's they can pacify 'em with a little bootleg vaudeville.

JOE. Can you beat that? (EDDIE *takes a large pair of shoes out of package and starts putting them on.*)

EDDIE. An' those picture punks is worse— Only last week I read where some guy's gonna make pictures smell. I'm seri-ous . . . They know what the public wants, too—so they're gonna make their pictures more and more like vaudeville. You'll see 'em . . . You'll hear 'em . . . You'll smell 'em.

JOSEY. I see plenty of 'em that smell.

JOE. Gee whiz.

EDDIE. I tell you . . . It's dog eat dog . . . But we're gonna beat 'em at their own game.

JOE. You bet we are. (EDDIE, *who now has on the lean-shoes, gets up, walks to* C. *of room and starts leaning this way and that. Laughing)* This is gonna be good.

EDDIE. Now, I'm on stage when the lights come up . . . An' Josey, you come on wavin' to somebody in the wings . . . but just when we're gonna bump, I lean outa the way.

JOSEY. *(Turning toward him from stove)* That's a funny piece of business.

JOE. How do you think 'em all up, Pop?

EDDIE. They just come to me . . . All right, Josey, let's go.

JOSEY. Can't we do it a little later, Eddie—I got all these things on the stove.

EDDIE. Never mind that—this is important— There's no time to lose.

JOSEY. Go ahead then—go ahead . . . I can do both.

EDDIE. Give me the first line.

JOSEY. Ah . . Why don't you look where you're goin'?

EDDIE. Why don't you go where you're lookin'? (JOE *laughs.*)

JOSEY. Oh, fresh . . . If I wasn't in a hurry, I'd sure give you a piece of my mind.

EDDIE. Can you spare it?

JOSEY. If I just knew where I was supposed to meet my brother—he'd fix you . . . Where's Clinton Street?

EDDIE. I don't know, I haven't got it . . . C'mon, Josey, give it a little ginger . . . you're dyin' on your feet.

JOSEY. Where was we?

EDDIE. "Where's Clinton Street? . . . I don't know . . . I haven't got it."

JOSEY. You don't know nothin', do you?

EDDIE. I ain't lost. (EDDIE *does an exaggerated lean and* JOE *laughs.* JOSEY *stops cooking and really works with him.*)

JOSEY. Oh, you men . . . Which street is this?

EDDIE. Watt Street.

JOSEY. This street.

EDDIE. Watt.

JOSEY. I just asked you.

EDDIE. I just told you.

JOSEY. What?

EDDIE. That's it, Watt.

JOSEY. What's it?

EDDIE. No, Watt's Watt.

JOSEY. That's what I said.

EDDIE. That's what I thought you said—Watt.

JOSEY. Oh, I give up.

EDDIE. Ain't that terrific, Josey?

JOE. I got a stomach-ache from laughin'.

JOSEY. That's a great improvement, all right . . . an' it should be sure-fire . . .

EDDIE. The other idea I got is even better.

JOE. Am I in it?

EDDIE. We're all in this one.

JOE. Hot-diggity.

JOSEY. *(Putting the last dish on table)* Come on, Joey, sit down and eat your supper.

JOE. All right, Mom—but I'm kinda too excited to eat. *(She pushes him down into a chair at table.)*

EDDIE. *(Holding sheet of music in his hand)* We'll knock 'em in the aisles with this one . . . An' it's made to order for you, Josey . . . Remember it?

JOSEY. Gee, will I ever forget it . . . That's one of the first numbers I ever did, Eddie— But you aren't gonna *use* it, are you?

EDDIE. It's so old—it's new . . . An' I got a production idea built around it that's a lulu.

JOE. *(Jumping up)* What do I do, Pop?

JOSEY. *(Pulling* JOE *back in his chair)* Why don't you sit down and eat, Eddie, while everything's hot?

EDDIE. How can I eat at a time like this? We only got five days to go—an' we gotta be prepared—we gotta be perfect. Let's go, gang.

JOE. *(Jumping up again)* I'm ready.

EDDIE. Sing the first verse, Josey, an' I'll direct you in the rest. Come here, Joe. *(Takes* JOE *over to mirror and starts talking to him a mile-a-minute in a low tone.* JOSEY *glances at music as she continues to eat)* Here, I'll put a spot on you, Josey . . . Now, let 'er rip. *(He flicks off wall switch, then tilts a bridge-lamp so that* JOSEY *is framed in its light.* EDDIE *and* JOE *can only be seen dimly.)*

JOSEY. *(Half singing)*
> Wonderful Pals are always hard to find
> Some folks have one,
> Some folks have none,
> I was alone for years, but fate was kind,
> And in the end,—
> Sent me a friend—
> Altho' he's not much higher than my knee—
> Still he's the greatest thing on earth to me.

(As she nears the end JOE *walks into the light. His hands and face are dirty, his shirt is hanging out, his hair is mussed and he is barefooted.)*

JOE. *(As she finishes)* Mama . . .

JOSEY. *(Looking up)* What in the name of God have you done to yourself? . . . Look at . . .

JOE. *(Quickly interrupting)* Go ahead, Mama . . . give me a spankin' . . . I deserve it—ever since dear Daddy died you worked your fingers to the bone to send me to school an' make me happy—an' all I ever do—is go out an' get in everybody's hair an' ruin my clothes—an' get myself all dirty . . . an' never do what you tell me . . . *(JOE's acting now reaches the tearful stage)* I'm just a disgrace to you . . . *(Bursts into tears. JOSEY puts arm around him.)*

EDDIE. Now take him on your knee, Josey—an' sing the chorus to him. *(JOSEY hesitates a moment, then goes into chorus and really sings it*)*

> Dirty-Hands, Dirty Face—
> Leads the neighbors a chase,
> But his smile is as cute as can be—
> Making noise, breaking toys,
> Always fights with the boys,
> But his eyes are a vision to see.
> And when my work is done,—
> Coming home to the setting sun,
> From the gate he starts to run,
> Then I kiss my boy—
> Dirty hands, Dirty face—
> Little Devil, they say—
> But to me—he's an angel of joy.

(JOSEY finishes and she just sits there, JOE in her arms.)

JOE. *(Jumping up)* It's the greatest idea you ever got, Pop. We'll gool 'em.

EDDIE. *(Who can only be dimly seen)* Get outa the way, Joey —an' watch ycur Old Man top that. *(EDDIE crawls into light on his hands and knees. His trouser legs are rolled up and he has improvised a diaper out of a tablecloth. He is bare from the waist up and his face is dirty. JOSEY sees him and explodes with laughter.)* Mama . . .

JOSEY. You're a scream.

EDDIE. Sing it to Snookums.

JOSEY. Climb up on my knee, Sonny Boy.

EDDIE. Marvelous, Josey . . . That line stays in . . . Why

---

*Copyright, 1923, by Clark & Leslie Songs, Inc., New York City, U.S.A.

didn't I think of it. *(He jumps up on her lap)* Take another chorus. *(*JOSEY *laughs again as she goes into second chorus.* EDDIE *looks cross-eyed, sucks his thumb, and does other bits of low comedy business keyed in with song.* JOSEY *twists his hair into a baby's peak. At line "Then I kiss my boy,"* EDDIE *gives her a long drawn-out and agonized kiss. At end of number he slides off her knees and takes a prat-fall. He "exits" bawling and rubbing his behind.* JOE *laughs all through this)* Now I ask you—how can we miss?

JOSEY. *(Still laughing)* Ed—you've never been funnier.

JOE. We'll murder 'em.

EDDIE. I never been this satisfied with the act all the years I'm in the business.

JOSEY. That's a honey of an idea.

EDDIE. All we need now is a snapper for the finish—an' we'll stop that show so cold—they won't be able to put on the picture.

JOE. Want to see my new routine now? *(*JOSEY *picks up contract and looks at it.)*

EDDIE. Let's see it, Joe— Hit while the iron's hot. *(*JOE *goes into routine and* EDDIE *watches him as he takes off diaper, lean shoes, etc. Finally he joins* JOE *in dance.)*

JOE. *(As they dance)* Gee, Pop, it's gonna be great playin' a real theater again, ain't it?

EDDIE. Just like comin' into the promised land. *(As their enthusiasm increases during rest of this exchange, their dance takes on a corresponding vigor.)*

JOE. No more roadhouses with everybody talkin' when you're doin' a number.

EDDIE. An' all them dishes rattlin'.

JOE. It's awful, ain't it?

EDDIE. Drunks queerin' your best laughs.

JOE. We won't have to worry about that any more, will we, Pop?

EDDIE. No, sir, Joey—that's ancient history.

JOSEY. *(Looking up from contract)* Why didn't you tell me the truth?

EDDIE. *(Stopping dance)* What do you mean?

JOSEY. This is only for one house . . .

EDDIE. You can't go by the contract, Josey . . .

JOSEY. You said you had a lot of time lined up . . .

EDDIE. We have if you just give us a chance.

JOSEY. An' I was chump enough to fall for it . . .

EDDIE. I tell you this time they're really gonna bring back vaudeville.

JOSEY. They was gonna bring it back before.

EDDIE. But vaudeville never had a chance in those dumps where they tried it . . . This is a class theater.

JOSEY. The last half—is the last half—why do you want to get us all hopped up again? *(A knock at door.)*

JOE. Mrs. Fuller! *(JOSEY opens door, revealing MOLLY and OTTO SHAEFFER. MOLLY is an expansive woman of 45. She is blonde and dressed fit to kill. She carries a large basket. OTTO is a small, beamish man of 52.)*

JOSEY. Molly and Otto! . . . Hello . . . Come in. *(They exchange greetings.)* Where you been keepin' yourself?

MOLLY. I was tellin' Otto yesterday—it's six months an' we don't see the Quinns—so here we are, Honey.

JOSEY. *(Taking MOLLY's arm and crossing with her to table)* An' you're a sight for sore eyes.

OTTO. We had a hard time getting here through that Decoration Day Parade. *(He hands JOE three small American flags set in a standard.)*

MOLLY. *(Handing JOSEY the basket)* Here—we brought you something. *(She sits at table.)*

JOSEY. Oh . . . Oh, look . . . You should'na done that . . A chicken . . . An' a ham . . . an' a bottle of whiskey . . . *(Impulsively she gives MOLLY a kiss)* You should'na done it.

MOLLY. Well, we just wanted to bring you a little something.

EDDIE. *(Crossing with OTTO to table)* It's nice of you, of course, but you didn't have to bring us anything . . .

JOSEY. If you just brought yourselves that's enough.

OTTO. We never forget what you done for me an' Molly that time in Omaha . . . Will we, Molly? *(Sits beside MOLLY.)*

MOLLY. An' we just thought we'd bring you something for old times.

EDDIE. *(To OTTO)* Why, if I hadn't knowed you from Adam we woulda done what we did . . . You gotta respect talent an' you got the greatest goat act—bar none—in the business. *(He also sits at table.)*

OTTO. Thanks . . . But just the same we never forget it.

JOSEY. C'mon an' we'll have a nip to the old days . . Run down to the drug store, Joe, an' get a bottle of soda. (JOE, *who has been playing with the American flags, puts them on the window sill.*)

JOE. Okay, Mom. (*She gives* JOE *some money and he runs out by fire escape.* MOLLY *and* OTTO *look puzzled.*)

EDDIE. It's quicker that way.

MOLLY. Will you ever forget Omaha?

JOSEY. Uh-uh.

OTTO. It don't seem like seventeen years, does it?

EDDIE. Is it seventeen years?

OTTO. Yep.

MOLLY. An' we thought we was bad off then . . . I wish we was back there.

JOSEY. Seventeen years . . . Joey wasn't even born then.

OTTO. No . . . You was doin' a double.

EDDIE. Omaha's where I first break in the tramp make-up.

OTTO. Was it?

EDDIE. Yeah . . . Omaha.

MOLLY. Say, 'member who was on the bill with us?

JOSEY. Who? . . . I forget.

MOLLY. Why, Jack Benny.

JOSEY. Was he?

EDDIE. Yeah, he was on that bill . . . in the number two spot, too.

JOSEY. Yes, he was . . . I remember now.

EDDIE. I got more laughs 'n he got, too.

OTTO. Did you hear him on the air Sunday?

MOLLY. (*Laughing*) He sure was a riot!

OTTO. An' that stooge he's got . . . (*To* JOSEY) Did you hear him?

JOSEY. No.

MOLLY. Ain't you got a radio, Honey?

EDDIE. (*Getting up*) No . . . An' we ain't gonna have one.

OTTO. What's the matter with having a radio?

EDDIE. I'll tell you what's the matter with it . . . Radio tries to kill our profession an' guys like Benny is traitors . . .

MOLLY. What do you mean?

EDDIE. When radio first came out they ain't got a thing to put on it . . . An' what happens—Benny, Cantor, Allen, Joe Cook, Burns and Allen, Frank Fay an' lots of others

flock to it an' right away radio's in an' vaudeville's dyin' . . .
An' vaudeville was good to them guys, too . . . They was
headliners . . . But they had to flock to radio . . . they're
fifth columnists . . .

MOLLY. I don't see how you figure that . . .

EDDIE. If them guys woulda ignored radio in the beginnin',
what could they a-put on the damn thing? Nothin' . . . Well,
maybe Chautauqua . . . An' radio woulda been just a pass-
in' fad . . . Like minature golf . . . An' vaudeville woulda
been vaudeville . . . But—no, they had to flock to it . . .

OTTO. You can't blame a guy for wantin' to eat . . .

EDDIE. They coulda et in vaudeville . . . If they stuck to it
. . . like you stuck to it—like I stuck to it . . .

OTTO. I don't know, Eddie . . .

EDDIE. But you'll know when I give you the good news . . .
Otto, you're just the guy I wanted to see . . . I can get you
the last half of next week . . . But, believe me, this is more
than just the last half . . . It's the opportunity beatin' at the
door.

OTTO. Thanks, Eddie, but you see . . .

EDDIE. I know what you're gonna say—"they tried it in other
places." But, where? Shootin' galleries— Scratch-houses—
Grinds . . . Remember the Stanwick out in the suburbs?
. . . It musta cost a million—but everything they try flops
. . . Bingo—Bank Night—Dishes—everything— Last week
I mosey out there an' all by myself I prove to them the only
thing can save them from ruin—is vaudeville. Why, with
great acts like ours it's gotta go . . . An' when it clicks
there, other houses'll try it—an' the public'll hear about it—
an' they'll realize what they been missin'—an' by God, they'll
make 'em bring back vaudeville . . .

OTTO. I hope you're right.

JOSEY. *(To* MOLLY) How're the goats?

MOLLY. Well . . .

JOSEY. Is anything wrong with 'em? (MOLLY *looks at* OTTO,
hesitates a moment, then blurts it out.)

MOLLY. We hadda sell the goats.

EDDIE. You what?

OTTO. *(Sadly)* Yeah . . . We hadda sell 'em . . .

EDDIE. Oh, that's awful . . . What made you do that?

MOLLY. They wasn't doin' nothin' . . .

OTTO. What Molly means is . . . Well . . . We didn't like to see 'em around . . .

EDDIE. I don't get it.

MOLLY. Otto means, we didn't need 'em . . . An' they wasn't doin' nothing . . . An' we hadda feed 'em . . .

OTTO. An' they looked at me so funny . . .

EDDIE. What is this? . . . Double-talk?

MOLLY. We ain't in vaudeville no more.

EDDIE. What do you mean?

OTTO. *(Sheepishly)* We're outa show business . . . for the time being.

MOLLY. *(Quickly)* For good.

EDDIE. *(Dumbfounded)* They sold the goats . . . They're outa vaudeville. *(He stands up.)*

JOSEY. *(Concerned)* How you gonna live? . . . An' you gettin' us presents . . . How could you?

MOLLY. Don't worry, Honey . . . We're better off'n we ever been . . . Otto's got himself a good job.

JOSEY. *(Interested)* What kinda job?

OTTO. I'm in a factory.

MOLLY. Forty-eight-seventy-five an' overtime. Just like the stage hands . . . Week in and week out.

JOSEY. Gee, that's great.

EDDIE. The goats is gone . . . An' you're in a factory! (ED-DIE *is flabbergasted. He flops into a chair and stares unbelieving at* OTTO.)

OTTO. It was a surprise to me, too—I never worked anything but the goats for twenty-five years.

MOLLY. An' they're gonna promote him.

JOSEY. What made you decide to get outa the business, Otto?

OTTO. Well, Josey, it's kinda funny . . . I was trampin' 'round the bookin' offices all one week . . . . An' I can't give the goats away . . .

MOLLY. You know Otto can't work the goats in club smokers and roadhouses, like you an' Eddie an' the kid . . .

OTTO. So I'm walking home an' . . .

MOLLY. An' we ain't got a thing . . . We owed rent an' . . .

OTTO. Do you want me to tell it—or do you want to tell it . . .

MOLLY. Go ahead . . .

OTTO. Well, I'm on the way home and I stop right in the middle of the street . . . An' I think why don't I just go home

. . . whack the goats over the head . . . Turn on the gas . . .
(He shrugs) Curtains.

JOSEY. You sure musta been down in the mouth.

MOLLY. We was.

OTTO. When I gets home I look at the goats a long time an'
finally I make up my mind . . . The goats gotta go . . .
The goats been good to me, but . . .

MOLLY. An' you wàs good to the goats.

OTTO. I know, Molly, I know, but just the same . . . Any-
ways, I make up my mind they gotta go . . . An' . . . *(He
has difficulty saying it)* An' I sold 'em to a farmer . . who
understands goats.

MOLLY. He was all broke up for a week.

OTTO. But we all gotta go sometime . . . An' it was the goats
or us . . . (EDDIE, *who has been squirming, now gets to his
feet.)*

EDDIE. You just done one thing wrong . . . When you get
the gas pipe idea . . . you shoulda come to me, see, an'
I'da fixed things right.

MOLLY. We didn't want to bother you—you got troubles, too.

EDDIE. *(To* OTTO) Here's what you shoulda done . . . You
shoulda left me get Brady, Dabinsky an' Zurkes together in
one office . . . They're the three worst stinkers of the bookin' agents . . . Right?

OTTO. Yeah . . . They're pretty lousy.

EDDIE. Then as I leave the office I give you the high sign an'
you're standing there with a gun in your hand.

OTTO. I don't get you.

EDDIE. *(Really worked up now)* An' you mosey in hiding the
gun an' ask Brady first—"Got anythin' for me an' the
goats?" He hates dumb acts, so he says "No" . . . Then you
ask Dabinsky. He don't like goats, either . . . Then you put
it to Zurkes . . . "Can you use me the last half?" An' the
answer is still "No" . . . So you whip out the gun an' let
the three of 'em have it . . . Then you put the gun to your
head an' blow out your own damn brains . . . *(He is in a
frenzy)* Then you know what happens? They take you down
to that actor's undertaker an' lay you out . . . An' the real
vaudeville artists all come by—look at you—raise their hats
an' say—"He had a lousy act, but, by God, he was the actors'
friend . . . "

MOLLY. *(Jumping to her feet)* You can't talk to Otto like that.

OTTO. *(Also rising)* I had as good an act as you got . . .

EDDIE. Brother, you're right where you belong now . . . In a factory— You had no damn right in vaudeville.

MOLLY. We don't have to listen to that kinda talk.

EDDIE. The truth hurts . . . don't it?

JOSEY. Eddie . . .

OTTO. We just come for a friendly visit . . . *(To* JOSEY*)* Has he been hittin' the bottle?

EDDIE. I ain't hittin' nothin'—an' we don't want no friendly visits from the likes of you.

MOLLY. I never been so insulted in my life. *(She crosses to door and* OTTO *follows.)*

OTTO. *(Near door)* You'll never see us again.

EDDIE. That's great . . . You stick where you belong . . . in the factory.

OTTO. Me an' the goats played better time than you ever played. *(*EDDIE *picks up basket and shoves it at* OTTO.*)*

EDDIE. *(Shouting)* I never shoulda helped you in Omaha . . . I shoulda let you starve . . . Take your lousy presents an' get out before I throw you out. *(They go. Speaking tube whistle is heard.* JOSEY *answers it. A voice is heard, but no words can be distinguished. Getting control of himself)* Who's that?

JOSEY. The man upstairs . . . He wants to sleep. *(*EDDIE *waves his arm at the ceiling.* JOSEY *crosses to table and starts removing dishes, etc.)*

EDDIE. Can you imagine the . . . Shows you how wrong you can be in people . . . *(*EDDIE, *who is in center of room, absentmindedly makes some comic faces.* JOE *enters window with soda water.)*

JOE. Where's Molly an' Otto?

JOSEY. They had to go.

JOE. What happened to the basket?

JOSEY. They took it with 'em.

JOE. Wouldn't you know—Indian givers!

JOSEY. You better go brush your teeth an' get ready for bed.

JOE. Already, Mom?

JOSEY. Yeah . . . I don't want you late for school again.

(She hands him a pair of sleepers) Now, hurry up and get into these. (JOE *starts—but seeing* EDDIE, *absentmindedly clowning, he stalls.)*

JOE. Figurin' out a new idea, Pop?

EDDIE. Huh? . . . No, Joey?—I was just practicin' a little.

JOE. Them other ideas was sure great, Pop—I was laughin' at 'em all the way to the store.

JOSEY. C'mon, Joey—do what I tell you, like a good little boy. (JOE *goes to door, opens it, peers up and down the hall, then exits.)*

EDDIE. Josey . . .

JOSEY. What?

EDDIE. You gotta admit I was right . . . Now don't you?

JOSEY. I'm ashamed of you . . . They're the best friends we got, too.

EDDIE. He shouldna sold the goats.

JOSEY. Sure he shoulda sold 'em.

EDDIE. Are you outa your head?

JOSEY. He done right gettin' a job, too.

EDDIE. What was right about it?

JOSEY. They needed room rent an' food—an' he got a job.

EDDIE. Yeah . . . in a factory—that's where the hell he belongs—not in vaudeville.

JOSEY. Maybe they just couldn't wait any longer?

EDDIE. What's the matter with you today, Josey?

JOSEY. Maybe they thought vaudeville's dead an' gonna stay dead.

EDDIE. But that's where they're wrong . . . That's why I hit the ceilin'. *(Door bursts open and* JOE *comes in crying.)*

JOSEY. What's the matter—did you hurt yourself?

JOE. It's Mrs. Fuller . . .

EDDIE. What did she do to you?

JOE. I was comin' outa the bath—an' she grabbed me and bawled me out . . . an' she said she was gonna throw us out . . .

JOSEY. *(Taking* JOE *in her arms)* Don't cry, Joey boy—she can't hurt you—I won't let her— Don't cry.

JOE. I'll be all right in a minute. (JOE *goes over to cot and flops down on it. He is wearing sleeper suit.)*

JOSEY. Poor Joey— Ed, you gotta do something . . .

EDDIE. I'll tell her where to get off . . . one of these days.

JOSEY. I don't care about myself—but I'm not gonna let him go through this . . . What's gonna become of him? He's behind in school . . . he don't want to learn—he thinks only of the damn act. *(Breaking)* I ain't gonna let him grow up in this lousy business . . . Eddie, you just gotta do something.

EDDIE. I am gonna do something.

JOSEY. Eddie, we're licked.

EDDIE. Don't, Josey—don't.

JOSEY. You gotta get a job—if Otto can get one—you can get one.

EDDIE. You mean—get a job outa vaudeville?

JOSEY. Oh, what's the use? *(She picks up her night things and goes out door. EDDIE stands looking after her, then becomes aware of JOE, who is still crying a little. He walks over and sits down on cot.)*

EDDIE. Don't cry, Joey.

JOE. I ain't cryin', Pop.

EDDIE. An' don't pay no attention to old feisty-face.

JOE. Why don't she like me, Pop? I never done anything to here . . . I was playin' out front yesterday with a kid from downstairs—an' she comes out an' shakes her fist at me and yells like anything . . . She never even shook her fist at the other kid . . .

EDDIE. She wasn't shakin' her fist at you, Joey.

JOE. Oh, yes, she was. *(He doubles up his fist and shakes it.)*

EDDIE. No, Joe, she was shakin' it at me.

JOE. But you wasn't even there, Pop.

EDDIE. I know, but she was kinda rehearsin' for me . . .

JOE. Oh . . .

EDDIE. How you comin' along in school?

JOE. *(Beginning to cry again)* I'm no good at school—an' I'm never gonna be no good at it.

EDDIE. But you gotta go to school.

JOE. All the teachers think I'm fresh.

EDDIE. But you must do fresh things to make them think you're fresh.

JOE. All right, Pop, if that's what you think, just listen to this . . . The other day the teacher's outa the room, see . . . An' all the kids got nothin' to do but study, so I told 'em a few gags, an' I'm just showin' 'em how to do a nip-up when

the teacher comes in an' asks me what do I think I'm doin'?
An' I said, "I'm teachin' the kids how to do a nip-up," an'
she says, "The idea!" An' I ask her can she do a nip-up . . .
an' she bawls me out an' says I'm fresh.

EDDIE. Nip-ups ain't so easy to do.

JOE. That's what I was tryin' to tell her, Pop.

EDDIE. But just the same, Joe, you gotta go to school some.

JOE. Did school ever help you—did they ever teach you dance
steps like "Over the Top" an' "Off to Buffalo" in school?

EDDIE. No, Joey, they don't . . . but . . .

JOE. Why, Pop, you're the greatest dancer in the world an'
you didn't even finish grammar school.

EDDIE. Yeah . . . but you don't want to grow up to an ignor-
amous like me.

JOE. Do you ever see any college guys in our business?

EDDIE. No, not many of 'em. (*He thinks*) I only 'member one
. . . when we was playin' Altoona . . . he was a singer . . .
an' they cancelled him after the first show an' moved me up
next to closin'.

JOE. (*Jumping up on his hands and knees in his excitement*)
There you are—that's what I been tryin' to tell Mom—but
she don't see it.

EDDIE. (*With some firmness*) Joe, you just gotta go to school
—some. (JOE *flops down on bed and cries again*) Don't, Joey
—don't . . . Look, if you stop cryin' I'll tell you what I'll
do . . .

JOE. What?

EDDIE. I'll get you a good piece of maple and make you a pair
of wooden clogs—just like mine.

JOE. Will you, honest—just like yours?

EDDIE. Yeah—just like mine.

JOE. (*Kissing him*) You're the greatest Pop in the world.

EDDIE. Now, you gonna stop cryin'?

JOE. You bet.

EDDIE. That's a good boy. Now go to sleep. (JOE *stretches out,
then after a second raises himself on one elbow.*)

JOE. Hey, Pop . . . (*He holds up two fingers in the shape
of a "V".*) "V" for Vaudeville.

EDDIE. Goodnight, son. (JOE *curls up and is quiet.* EDDIE *turns
out all the lights except the one near bed. He walks around
the room, then stops and looks at* JOE. *He is still looking at*

him when JOSEY *returns, wearing a kimono. Without a word* JOSEY *goes over to* JOE'S *cot, sees that he is all right, then crosses to folding bed, pulls it down and gets in.* EDDIE *looks at her, then moves over to folding bed)* Josey . . .

JOSEY. What is it, Ed?

EDDIE. I can't get outa vaudeville . . . It's my profession.

JOSEY. Oh, don't start it again—my head's splittin'.

EDDIE. I gotta stick in vaudeville . . . It's in my blood . . . Josey, our break'll come.

JOSEY. It never come when there was vaudeville . . . We was always a flop.

EDDIE. Josey, you don't know what you're sayin'.

JOSEY. *(Quietly)* We was always gonna play the Palace . . . we never did—. Now there ain't no Palace . . . We was alway gonna play Big Time— We played honkey-tonks . . . One night stands . . . Always worryin' about the last half. We don't belong in vaudeville . . . Neither . . . We never belonged. *(Starting to cry again)* I wish to God I could get a job . . . Chambermaid—scrubwoman—anything . . . I don't care. *(She buries her head in pillows.)*

EDDIE. Josey . . . Josey . . . *(She doesn't answer.* EDDIE *looks at her, then walks slowly to window and looks out. After a while, he turns and looks at gas stove. He goes over and fools with the handle for a second, then turns it on and gas is heard. He turns it off, then goes to window and closes it. Whispering)* Josey . . . *(She doesn't answer or move. He shrugs grotesquely, almost like a clown, then goes quickly to stove and turns on gas again. He walks to window and leans against frame, gazing outside. He raises one hand and rests it near poster bearing the billing: "THE THREE DANCING QUINNS." As gas continues to pour out of stove, he lowers his head. In a moment, he looks up and as he does, his eyes fall on poster and he runs his hand over the line, "THE THREE DANCING QUINNS." Suddenly, he stops in the act of doing this and snaps his fingers. Then quickly opens window. With feverish excitement)* Josey . . . Josey . . . Wake up! *(He runs to stove, shuts off gas, then hurrying to cot awakens* JOE) Wake up, Joe . . . Wake up!

JOE. What's the matter, Pop?

EDDIE. I got that snapper for the finish of the act.

JOE. *(Jumping up)* Oh, boy!

EDDIE. Instead of our regular closing song, sing that new tune I taught you and then watch the fireworks.

JOE. *(Facing audience and singing)* "My Country 'Tis of Thee, etc." *(EDDIE runs to window and grabs three American flags which MOLLY and OTTO brought.)*

JOSEY. *(Sitting up in bed)* What in the name of God are you doing now?

EDDIE. *(Helping JOSEY out of bed and sticking American flag in her hand)* Come on, Josey. *(He hurries her over beside JOE, who has gone right on singing)* I got a patriotic finish for the act that'll send those peasants outa that theater demanding they bring back vaudeville. *(He hands JOE a flag and joins him in song. JOSEY hesitates for a second, then shaking her head slightly joins them in song. All three now face the audience and sing "My Country 'Tis of Thee" at the top of their lungs while furiously waving their flags.)*

CURTAIN

GONE TOMORROW

CHARACTERS

PETER MULDOON
JENNY MULDOON
WILLIE MULDOON, *their son*
UNCLE HUGHIE
JERRY CANAVAN, *a friend of the Muldoons*
MR. BIGELOW, *a visitor*
MRS. LACEY, *a next-door neighbor*

SCENE: *The kitchen in the Muldoon home in the so-called Hell's Kitchen district of New York's West Side. There is a large table* C., *and* U.L. *a large kitchen coal stove. On the wall to* L. *of stove are several shelves containing pots, pans, bottles, etc. A doorway* C., *which leads to upper part of house. A frayed curtain takes the place of a door. A door to* R. *leading to street and one* L. *opening on a back-yard.*
MRS. MULDOON, *a tall, broad-hipped, broad-bosomed woman in her early fifties, is standing by upstairs door, her head to one side, listening.*
MRS. LACEY, *a white-haired little woman wearing a shawl, is seated at table. She intently watches* MRS. MULDOON, *then leans forward in her chair.*

MRS. LACEY. Can you hear anything? (MRS. MULDOON *shakes head.*) The doctor must be examin' him.
MRS. MULDOON. It wouldn't take him this long. You could examine Uncle Hughie in two minutes.
MRS. LACEY. No, there isn't much to him even for a man of eighty. The last time I seen him on the street I was astonished how he ud wasted away to almost nothing. He reminded me of an uncle I used to have that kep shrinkin' an' shrinkin' the same way until the last five years he was alive he got all his clothes in the boys' department an' when he died his casket was so small you had to look twice to be certain he

wasn't a little lad in long britches. *(There is an insistent
banging and both women look up. In a moment* MRS. MUL-
DOON *hurries to* L. *door.)*

MRS. MULDOON. *(Shouting)* Willie, come in here quick. (WIL-
LIE MULDOON, *aged fifteen, runs on stage.)* Hurry upstairs
and see what he wants. (WILLIE *goes.* MRS. MULDOON *returns
to table.)*

MRS. LACEY. *(Looking apprehensively up at ceiling as banging grows in volume)* Has he always been such a bitter man?

MRS. MULDOON. *(Shaking head)* When he first come to this
country, he was pleasant as Punch, an' always referred to me
an' Mr. Muldoon as his favorite newphew an' niece. *(Banging suddenly stops.)*

MRS. LACEY. Well, you certainly wasn't his favorite since you
been living here.

MRS. MULDOON. It was when we moved from the big house
on Third Street the trouble began. He always thought we just
moved here to spite him out of his meetings.

MRS. LACEY. What do you mean by his meetings?

MRS. MULDOON. Well, the house we lived in in Third Street
was twice the size of this and he had the whole top floor.
Practically every night of the week he'd have a gang of his
old Fenian friends up there, an' they made such a racket
shouting 'Up the Rebels,' 'Down with England' an' the like
that the whole neighborhood got up in arms over the noise
and we finally had to vacate the premises. An' when we re-
fused to let him go on with his confabs here in this house,
he turned on us just like that, accusin' us of every crime
under the sun against the Irish Republic.

MRS. LACEY. *(After a pause)* I don't for the life of me see
how he makes his wants beknownst to you if he don't talk
to you . . . specially now he's flat on his back.

MRS. MULDOON. Oh, it's an aggravatin' rigamarole we got to
go through. He tells me son Willie what he wants; Willie
tells me; I get it for him if I'm able; I give it to Willie; Willie gives it to him; then half the time he don't want it after
he gets it. *(Door is slammed offstage.)*

MRS. LACEY. There goes the Doctor. (WILLIE *enters* R.)

MRS. MULDOON. What did Dr. Boyle have to say this time?

WILLIE. He said he didn't think Uncle Hughie could last
much longer, an' if he gets any worse in the night, phone him

an' he'll come right over. (MRS. MULDOON *sits at table.* WILLIE *goes off* L.)

MRS. LACEY. *(Patting* MRS. MULDOON *on shoulder)* There, there, don't take it so hard, dearie.

MRS. MULDOON. The thought of a funeral in the house is very disturbin'.

MRS. LACEY. What is to be will be. We all got to go some time an' if you force yourself to look at funerals as necessary evils, they ain't as bad as they might be . . . why, I seen the time I ud weep an' wail at the very idear of one, but now I consider it me duty to participate in as many as possible so's to steel myself agin the thought of goin' when me own time comes . . . I'm also gettin' so's I derive an increasin' comfort from a wake. You're always sure to see a lot of your own kind includin' many old friends that don't get out an' around so much any more except to such occasions. An' if you should be carried away be all the pious excitement, there's always a drop or two to soften your sorrow . . . (MRS. MULDOON *holds out her hand for silence.*)

MRS. MULDOON. Is that him fidgettin' around up there?

MRS. LACEY. I didn't hear nothin'.

MRS. MULDOON. Go up an' peek in the door an' see if he's needin' anything. He won't let me come near him. (MRS. LACEY *goes to* C. *door and pulling curtain aside, goes upstairs. In a moment there is a thud and* MRS. LACEY *cries out.* MRS. MULDOON *runs to upstairs doorway just as* MRS. LACEY *reappears.)* What happened?

MRS. LACEY. I never been so humiliated in me life . . . I stuck me head in the door, he sat up in bed, called me a dirty Black an' Tanner and threw a pot at me.

MRS. MULDOON. *(Shaking head)* He must of thought it was me.

MRS. LACEY. There's a demon in that old man an' that's all there is to it, there's a demon in him. An' what you should do right this instant, atheist or no atheist, is send for the priest. *(Door is heard opening and closing.)*

MRS. MULDOON. *(Starting)* That can't be Mr. Muldoon. It isn't five-thirty, is it?

MRS. LACEY. I hope it ain't. I ain't got a thing on the stove. (PETER MULDOON, *fifty-five, a tall, thin man wearing a streetcar conductor's uniform, enters. He absently pulls at a long,*

*drooping moustache and appears unaware of the women as
he walks over to shelves by stove. He fusses around, apparently looking for something.)*

MRS. MULDOON. Ain't you home kind of early today?

MULDOON. *(Looking at his watch)* No, I'm right on schedule . . . where's me pipe?

MRS. MULDOON. It's where you put it, I suppose.

MULDOON. *(Turning and staring at his wife)* It's not where
I put it. If it was where I put it, it ud be where I was just
lookin', 'cause that's where I put it.

MRS. LACEY. If you need me for anything, dearie, bang on
the wall. *(She goes.)*

MULDOON. What was she snoopin' around about?

MRS. MULDOON. She wasn't snoopin' around about anything.
She came over to see if she could help me.

MULDOON. *(Jerking his thumb toward ceiling)* How is he?

MRS. MULDOON. Worse. The Doctor was just here an' he said
he ud be lucky to pull through the night.

MULDOON. Is he unconscious?

MRS. MULDOON. Not so's you could notice it. He's on'y just
after throwin' a pot at Mrs. Lacey.

MULDOON. There! I knowed she was snoopin' around. She
has no right to be there.

MRS. MULDOON. She has every right. I sent her up to see how
he was. (MULDOON *removes his coat and hangs it on hook
near upstairs door; then stands there listening.)*

MULDOON. *(Jerking his thumb toward ceiling again)* Did he
say anything to Willie since the Doctor went?

MRS. MULDOON. Willie went out.

MULDOON. Why wasn't Willie here? I commanded him not
to leave the premises at an important time like this. You
should of watched out he was here an' stayed here.

MRS. MULDOON. I can't watch upstairs, downstairs an' both
doors at the same time.

MULDOON. Supposin' he passed away before tellin' Willie
where he hides what money he's got left . . . tricky as he is
he ud have us huntin' high an' low for it all over the house
like a pack of bloodhounds.

MRS. MULDOON. It's a pity all you got on your mind is his
money.

MULDOON. *(Extracting bottle from shelf)* It ain't all I got on me mind at all. But what he's got left we're entitled to without fussin' an' worryin' about that as well as about him. *(Holds up bottle)* Somebody's been at this.

MRS. MULDOON. You've certainly come home with a sweet disposition tonight. *(She goes to stove and starts her cooking preparations.)*

MULDOON. Just you take care of your own disposition. Don't worry about me. *(He drains bottle.* WILLIE *enters* L.)

WILLIE. Hello, Pop.

MULDOON. Never mind the Pop, where you been?

WILLIE. I been out.

MULDOON. Damn it, I know you been out, but I told you to be in.

WILLIE. Uncle Hughie sent me on an errand.

MULDOON. What did he send you to do?

MRS. MULDOON. When did he send you? *(She moves over to* WILLIE.)

WILLIE. Just before the Doctor came.

MULDOON. What did he send you to do, I asked you? Answer me when I ask you.

WILLIE. Well, Mom asked me something.

MULDOON. Never mind what Mom asked you, *I'm* askin' you. What did he send you to do?

WILLIE. He sent me to phone Mr. Bigelow.

MULDOON. Who is Mr. Bigelow?

WILLIE. I don't know.

MULDOON. A fine son you raised!

MRS. MULDOON. What did he ask you to ask Mr. Bigelow?

WILLIE. He asked me to ask him to come over here as quick as he could.

MRS. MULDOON. Did Uncle Hughie say who he was?

WILLIE. No, he just asked me to ask him to come over, and he said he would.

MULDOON. The old sinner is up to some kind of spiteful treachery.

MRS. MULDOON. Did you do anything else for Uncle Hughie?

WILLIE. *(Nodding)* I delivered a letter for him.

MULDOON. Who'd you deliver it to?

WILLIE. The Presbyterian Hospital.

MULDOON. *(Pounding table)* That's the limit . . . now he's going to become a Protestant atheist!

MRS. MULDOON. *(Shocked)* Why didn't you tell me you was deliverin' a message to the Presbyterians?

WILLIE. You never asked me.

MULDOON. None of your lip.

WILLIE. I've been deliverin' notes to the Presbyterian Hospital for Uncle Hughie all month now.

MRS. MULDOON. It's the strangest thing I ever heard, him writing to them.

MULDOON. Trouble always comes in bunches. *(Front doorbell rings.)*

MRS. MULDOON. There, that's this Mr. Bigelow now . . . Bring him in here, Willie, an' be quick about it. (WILLIE *hurries off through door* R.)

MULDOON. I'll damn soon find out what this Bigelow business is. (MRS. MULDOON *edges over to her husband's side and they both stand at rigid attention.* WILLIE *reappears, followed by* JERRY CANAVAN, *a withered-up little old man. He stops just inside door, tapping top of his derby.* WILLIE *sits on chair down* R.)

MRS. MULDOON. *(Tartly)* Oh, it's you again. *(She returns to her work at stove.)*

MULDOON. What do you mean comin' in the front door an' upsettin' people like that?

JERRY. The back gate was locked. *(Rolls his eyes toward ceiling)* I just wanted to find out how the old boy was doin'.

MRS. MULDOON. I've already told you three times today how he's doin'.

JERRY. I just seen the Doctor leave an' I thought maybe I could be a help to you. That was all.

MULDOON. He's sinkin' fast.

JERRY. God rest him. *(He respectfully raises his derby for a moment, then puts it back.)*

MRS. MULDOON. *(Suddenly)* Say, Jerry, did you ever know a Mr. Bigelow?

JERRY. We was boyhood chums together. (MRS. MULDOON *leaves stove, hurries to* JERRY.)

MULDOON. Now we're gettin' somewheres. You come at just the right time, Jerry. *(Indicates a chair for* JERRY; *both sit.)*

MRS. MULDOON. What does he do, Jerry, an' how does he come to know Uncle Hughie?

JERRY. Well, he was a hand riveter in the ship-yards but I

don't think he ever knowed your Uncle Hughie, because the Bigelow I knowed passed away a year or two years before your Uncle Hughie come to this country . . . but why did you ask?

MULDOON. None of your damn business.

MRS. MULDOON. Now, Peter, that's no way to be talkin' to Jerry. It's not his fault if he don't know the same Mr. Bigelow. *(To* JERRY*)* You'll have to forgive us, we're all jumpy as cats.

JERRY. I understand, I understand. You wouldn't be human if you wasn't at a time like this. Maybe this'll steady you. *(He pulls out a bottle and places it on table.)*

MULDOON. *(Eyeing bottle)* I didn't mean to lose me temper.

JERRY. It's no wonder you did, Peter, with the burden you got on your shoulders.

MULDOON. Give us some glasses here. (MRS. MULDOON *goes to shelves just as an insistent banging begins on floor above.)* There he goes agin.

MRS. MULDOON. Go up an' see what he wants, Willie. (WILLIE *runs out upstairs as banging increases.)*

JERRY. He certainly makes a hell of a hullabaloo for a man who's sinkin' fast, don't he?

MRS. MULDOON. Sometimes it's worse. I hope he don't bring the plaster down on us agin. *(Banging stops.* MRS. LACEY *dashes in* L.)

MRS. LACEY. *(Breathlessly)* I knew it ud come. I was standin' by the stove when all of a sudden I had a sure sign . . . I went hot an' cold an' I had a feelin' like there was a flight of sparrows goin' up an' down me backbone. Then the bangin' commenced an' I was sure.

MULDOON. What the hell is she ravin' about now?

MRS. LACEY. About him goin'.

MULDOON. He ain't gone yet.

MRS. LACEY. *(To* MRS. MULDOON) Then why was you bangin' on the wall?

MRS. MULDOON. *(Looking toward ceiling)* It was him that was bangin'.

MRS. LACEY. Well, if I knowed that's how it was you wouldn't of found me buttin' in like this.

MRS. MULDOON. You're not buttin' in. Peter, tell her she's not buttin' in.

MULDOON. Will you, for God's sake stop puttin' words in me mouth? She's the one who's accusin' herself of buttin' in.

MRS. MULDOON. Don't pay any attention to him. He's been cross as a crow ever since he come in.

MRS. LACEY. *(To* MRS. MULDOON*)* You know I ain't in the habit of buttin' in where I'm not wanted.

MULDOON. Will you please stop harpin' on that! Nobody's said you was buttin' in.

MRS. MULDOON. Sit you down, Mrs. Lacey, an' have a drink with us. (MRS. MULDOON *fills glasses.* MRS. LACEY *sits at table.)*

JERRY. Better days . . . an' an easy time of it for the old boy. *(They drink.* WILLIE *comes downstairs.)*

MULDOON. What did he want?

WILLIE. He wanted to know who rung the bell.

MRS. MULDOON. He wants to know everything that goes on. He never misses a trick. (WILLIE *goes off* L. MULDOON *pounds table.)* What's come over you now?

MULDOON. I forgot to ask Willie to ask him why he wrote to the Presbyterians, an' if I send him up now agin the old codger'll suspicion it's us that wants to know, and he'll shut his trap tighter'n a clam.

MRS. LACEY. Why in heaven's name did he write to the Presbyterians?

MRS. MULDOON. We wish we knew.

JERRY. He must of been delirious.

MRS. LACEY. Sometimes just before the end comes they act very peculiar. Me mother used to tell a tale about her father when he was right on the edge. He asked his wife, me grandmother, to make him a dish of stew . . . she was a very fine cook. But before she could get it in a pot an' on the stove, he was gone.

JERRY. Peter, have you done any thinkin' about the funeral itself?

MULDOON. I been able to think of nothin' else. It's been worryin' me days on the car an' worryin' me nights in me dreams.

JERRY. *(Enthusiastically)* Well, your worries is over, Peter, because I got just the man for you. It's Mr. Danzinger. He's a new undertaker in the neighborhood but he's the best man, bar none, in the whole city. When he takes over you've never a care. He don't miss a detail. Everything from beginning to end is under his own personal management. He presses their clothes, shaves 'em, puts the right amount of color in their cheeks an' all that. In additional, he provides plenty of extra chairs for the wake an' he himself rehearses the pallbearers until they're letter perfect. An' he's got a brand new hearse that's the biggest one I ever seen in me life.

MULDOON. I never heard of him before.

MRS. LACEY. What's the matter with Mr. Coyle's undertaking? You'd have to go some to beat him.

JERRY. Coyle ain't one, two, three with this man. They just ain't in the same class. Why, I'm not exaggeratin' when I make the statement Danzinger's corpses, on the whole, look fifty percent more natural than any other embalmer we got in town.

MRS. LACEY. I ain't seen none of his work yet, but if it was me I ud have nobody but Mr. Coyle. Why, he done such a pretty job on old Pete Kenigan that he looked better dead than he ever did alive. An' when I presented meself at the wake it wouldn't of surprised me a bit if he ud sat up in his casket an' thanked me for comin'.

MULDOON. How's this fellow about price, Jerry?

JERRY. Very reasonable, very reasonable. He . . .

MRS. MULDOON. (Interrupting) Before you get into that, what are you goin' to do about gettin' a priest to him?

MULDOON. One thing at a time, one thing at a time!

MRS. MULDOON. That's just what I'm doin', one thing at a time. Because if you don't get a priest to him an' get that crazy atheism out of his head, you'll not be havin' a church funeral an' you'll not be buryin' him in church ground.

MRS. LACEY. She's right.

MRS. MULDOON. You bet I am, an' I'm goin' to get the priest right now.

MULDOON. You'll do nothin' of the kind.

MRS. MULDOON. An' why won't I?

MULDOON. You know how he feels about the priests an' wouldn't it be a fine thing if just when Father Malone walked in his room the angry shock of seein' a cassock took the old heathen away that second. Wouldn't that set the tongues of the Protestant busybodies a-waggin'?

JERRY. It certainly would that.

MRS. MULDOON. All right, I'll ask you a question then. Are

you goin' to let him die an atheist in this house? That'll set some tongues a-waggin', too.

MULDOON. If it isn't one tormentin' thing it's something worse.

MRS. LACEY. Why don't you wait'll the breath goes out of his body entirely an' his heart quiets down completely, then rush somebody over for the priest?

MRS. MULDOON. It'll be too late then.

MULDOON. There's no use arguin' with a corpse.

JERRY. I think I got the solution of your problem. Why don't you wait till he gets about half-unconscious near the end, then send for the priest? The old boy won't have the strength then to kick up much of a fuss.

MRS. MULDOON. I think he's talkin' sense, Peter. *(She walks to stove and continues with her cooking.)*

MULDOON. Yes, that's the best idear we got so far . . . thanks, Jerry.

JERRY. Don't mention it. Glad to be of help.

MRS. LACEY. If it was me, I wouldn't trust him half unconscious or three-quarters unconscious.

MULDOON. Nobody's askin' you to trust anybody.

MRS. LACEY. Well, if he ud throw a pot at me, an innocent bystander, I wouldn't put nothin' past him.

JERRY. Peter, you was askin' about Danzinger's prices. Well, I think I can safely predict that Danzinger'll make you the best bargain, considerin' all he gives you, of any other embalmer hereabouts.

MRS. LACEY. I still say Mr. Coyle ud be better, specially if you have to pay for it yourself.

MULDOON. Who said we was goin' to pay for it? He's goin' to pay for it with the money he's been miserin' ever since he come to this country . . . *(Suddenly becoming alarmed)* What ever put such a thought as that in your head? Have you heard anything? Speak up, woman!

MRS. LACEY. No, I ain't heard nothin' . . . But I was just thinkin' when I was a girl we had a cousin that went out to Montana to be a minin' man an' everybody thought when he died we was all goin' to be rich. Well, he died an' afterwards one day a package come to the house an' everybody thought it was gold nuggets. But when we opened it up all there was was a set of books, two suits too big for anybody in the family, some shirt dickies, a mouth organ, six celluloid collars, a set of iron dumbbells an' some other things I forget now. It come C.O.D., too.

MULDOON. *(Stunned)* How do we know he's got any money left to leave us? How do we know he ain't spent it all an' left us to pay for his funeral?

MRS. LACEY. I didn't mean to be buttin' in, but the memory just crossed me mind an' I thought I ud better tell you.

MRS. MULDOON. Contrary as he is, I don't think he'd leave us in such a pickle.

MULDOON. Well, if he does, the atheists can bury him, or they can bury him in Potter's Field for all I give a damn.

MRS. MULDOON. *(Turning toward him)* How can you say such a thing?

JERRY. Don't lose your temper, Peter, don't lose your temper.

MULDOON. Don't lose me temper, is it? For twenty-seven years I've put up with the old reprobate's bickerin' an' backbitin', put up with him getting us booted out of the big house on Third Street with his Sein Fein shindigs, put up with him never sayin' a word to me nor the Missus two years handrunnin' now, put up with him brandin' us turncoats an' informers all over the neighborhood, put up with him settin' fire to the bed when he goes to sleep with his pipe lit, an' now I'm to put up with payin' for his funeral out of me own pocket, an' you got the gall to tell me not to lose me temper! Well, he's played his last spiteful shenanigan on this bucko, an' I repeat it, they can bury him in Potter's Field for all I give a damn.

MRS. MULDOON. *(Crossing to MULDOON)* They'll do nothin' of the kind. Come what may he's goin' to have a proper funeral.

JERRY. Oh, there's no two ways about it, you're duty bound to bury him decent.

MULDOON. I said I'll pay for no funeral.

MRS. MULDOON. You don't know for sure we'll have to pay for it, but if we do you can make up your mind that he's goin' to have a proper funeral.

MRS. LACEY. An' that's why I ud stick to Mr. Coyle, because if you haven't got the cash handy he'll credit you till you can take care of it. The Delaneys was five years, two months, payin' for their grandfather with never a word of reproach from Mr. Coyle.

JERRY. *(Furious)* Danzinger'll give you all the credit you want, too.

MRS. LACEY. How do you know he will?

JERRY. Because I work for him, that's how I know. (MRS. LACEY *and the* MULDOONS *jump to their feet.)*

MRS. MULDOON. You WHAT?

JERRY. *(Sheepishly)* Well . . . what I mean to say is, I'm sort of learnin' the trade.

MRS. MULDOON. At last it dawns on me why you been around three times today askin' how he was doin'.

MRS. LACEY. He ought to be ashamed of himself, waitin' like a buzzard for the old boy to go cold.

MULDOON. By God, if I'd knowed that's what you was up to, you'd never caught me wettin' me lips with your whiskey. You've sunk pretty low to be pimpin' for an embalmer.

JERRY. I'm doin' nothin' of the kind, Peter. I knew the predicament you was in an' where's the harm in recommendin' the best man, bar none.

MRS. LACEY. An' gettin' yourself a fat cut in the bargain.

MULDOON. No wonder you was boostin' him to the skies. *(Doorbell rings.)*

MRS. MULDOON. That's Mr. Bigelow this time an' no mistake. *(She hurries to door* L. *and throws it open)* Willie! Come in here!

MRS. LACEY. Who is Mr. Bigelow?

MULDOON. Whoever he is, he's not comin' in to this house.

MRS. MULDOON. An' why won't he?

MULDOON. Because he's a friend of Uncle Hughie's an' he's an atheist, an' one of them in the house at a time is enough.

MRS. MULDOON. How do you know he's a friend of Uncle Hughie's? An' how do you know he's an atheist?

MULDOON. I feel it in me bones, that's how I know, an' he's not comin' into this house.

MRS. MULDOON. Will you use your head an' keep your mouth shut till we find out what he's up to?

MRS. LACEY. She's right, Mr. Muldoon, you ought to have a look at him. (WILLIE *enters* L.)

WILLIE. What do you want, Mom?

MRS. MULDOON. Never mind, I'll go meself . . . *(To* MUL-

DOON) Now keep your shirt on. *(She crosses to door* R. *and exits.* WILLIE *sits on chair above door* R.)

MULDOON. I've stood all of his trickery I'm goin' to stand.

JERRY. Take it easy, man, take it easy, an' I'll ferret around an' see if this Mr. Bigelow knowed the same Bigelow 1 knowed. (MRS. MULDOON *reappears, followed by a well-dressed elderly man who carries a brief-case.)*

MRS. MULDOON. This is me husband, Mr. Peter Muldoon, the sick man's only nephew, an' that's Mrs. Lacey, our next-door neighbor, an' Jerry Canavan, an' this is me son. Stand up, Willie. (WILLIE *stands up and sits right down again.)*

BIGELOW. How do you do?

JERRY. I didn't get the name.

MRS. MULDOON. It's Mr. Bigelow.

JERRY. Oh, Bigelow, is it? Well, it's certainly a small world. I used to have a friend named Bigelow. He's dead about sixteen years, God rest him. I wonder if you was any kin to him, both havin' the same name? He was called Charley Bigelow an' he worked in the shipyards.

BIGELOW. I'm afraid not.

JERRY. I was just wonderin'. It's an odd kind of name you don't hear very often nowadays. *(Banging begins again on floor above.)*

MRS. MULDOON. *(Anxiously looking at ceiling)* I think you'd better go up to him, Mr. Bigelow. He's expectin' you. Step over this way, please. *(She pulls curtain aside)* His room is at the head of the stairs just to the left. (MR. BIGELOW *bows and exits through* C. *door.)*

MULDOON. Psst . . . folley him upstairs, Jenny, an' see if you can hear what goes on. (MRS. MULDOON *tiptoes up stairs after* MR. BIGELOW.)

JERRY. He was kind of snippety, wasn't he, when I asked him about Charley Bigelow? (MRS. LACEY *and* MULDOON *move very close to him.)*

MRS. LACEY. I didn't like his looks at all.

MULDOON. We was just confabbin' with an atheist an' I know what I'm alkin' about.

JERRY. I think maybe we was at that. *(A thud upstairs and* MRS. MULDOON *cries out.)*

MRS. LACEY. I knew that was goin' to happen. *(She starts*

toward door L. MRS. MULDOON *hurries downstairs with her hand to her head.)*

MULDOON. What happened to you?

MRS. MULDOON. I went up like you tell me an' I'm standin' there by the door an' the old codger must of seen me through the crack because he quick lifts up his cane an' shoves the door shut right on me head.

MULDOON. Here, Jerry, you hustle up there an' see what you can overhear.

JERRY. Not me, Peter. This is a private family affair an' I've no right to be snoopin' an' sneakin' around upstairs listenin' in on a dyin' man's last words.

MRS. LACEY. *(Who is now at the door, all set to make a quick getaway)* Don't look at me. I ducked out of the way of one pot an' I'll not duck out of the way of another.

MRS. MULDOON. Willie, go up there quick an' see what you can hear. (WILLIE *goes to* C. *door and exits.* MRS. LACEY *stifles a cry.)*

MULDOON. What ails you?

MRS. LACEY. A terrible thought just crossed me mind.

MULDOON. *(Sitting at table)* There she goes again. (JERRY *also sits at table.)*

MRS. MULDOON. What is it, Mrs. Lacey?

MULDOON. Go on an' say it. It can't be any worse than some of the other things you've said.

MRS. LACEY. I was just thinkin', supposin' this Mr. Bigelow ain't an atheist after all, supposin' he was a Presbyterian minister?

JERRY. By God, he could be at that! There's no way of tellin' one by his collar an' look at the way he acted when I asked him about Charley Bigelow.

MRS. MULDOON. We'd never live it down.

MULDOON. Well, that settles it. If he's goin' to comport with Presbyterians in this house the Presbyterians can bury him.

MRS. LACEY. I didn't mean to be buttin' in, but all of a sudden I went hot an' cold an' I was sure he was a Presbyterian.

JERRY. An' I agree with you.

MRS. MULDOON. Here he comes back down again.

MULDOON. Let him come. An' I'm goin' to ask him right to his face, an' if he says he is, minister or no minister, you're goin' to see some fur fly around here. (BIGELOW *enters through* C. *door.)*

MRS. MULDOON. How is he, Mr. Bigelow?

BIGELOW. He seems to be as well as could be expected.

MULDOON. Did you finish your business with me uncle?

MRS. MULDOON. He isn't gettin' sort of half-unconscious, is he?

BIGELOW. No, he appears to be in full possession of his faculties.

MULDOON. I said, did you finish your business with me uncle?

BIGELOW. Yes. As you probably know, I'm Mr. Muldoon's lawyer and he wanted to make a change in a will he had me draw up some months ago . . . *(To* MRS. MULDOON) Here is my card. Please get in touch with me when the time comes.

MRS. MULDOON. Thank you, I will.

BIGELOW. Good day. *(He leaves.)*

MULDOON. He's made a will!

MRS. MULDOON. *(To* MRS. LACEY) An' you was so sure he was a Presbyterian!

MRS. LACEY. Well, he certainly looked like one, didn't he, Jerry?

JERRY. Don't get me mixed up in this. It was all your idea.

MULDOON. He must have something left to leave or he wouldn't be makin' a will. An' he's got nobody else but us to leave it to.

JERRY. Your worries is all over now. (WILLIE *enters through* C. *door.)*

MRS. MULDOON. What went on, Willie?

MULDOON. How much did he say he was leavin' us in his will?

WILLIE. Mr. Bigelow told Uncle Hughie . . . or I mean Uncle Hughie told him . . .

MULDOON. Are you tryin' to torment me agin?

MRS. MULDOON. Will you give the boy a chance? Go on, Willie, what did Uncle Hughie say?

WILLIE. I think he told him he was to give Pop eight hundred and fourteen dollars. (WILLIE *crosses to chair above door* R. *and sits down.)*

MULDOON. Eight hundred and fourteen dollars?

MRS. LACEY. That's an awful lot of money.

JERRY. Why, it's a regular fortune.

MULDOON. *(After a pause)* Maybe he ain't such a spiteful old codger after all. *(He sits at table.)*

MRS. MULDOON. You're pipin' a different tune now, ain't you?

MULDOON. We can all make a mistake, Jenny.

MRS. MULDOON. While you was runnin' him down to beat the band, there he was up there thinkin' of us. *(She crosses to stove.)*

MULDOON. I wasn't runnin' him down exactly . . . all I was hintin' at was he had his little faults same as anybody else. Nobody is perfect.

JERRY. Spoken like a man, Peter. *(He also sits down.)*

MULDOON. Well, it's no more than the truth.

MRS. LACEY. We all got to forgive an' forget. *(She sits at table.)*

MULDOON. *(Sadly)* I got nothin' to forgive him for. He never done me any harm . . . He led his life the best way he could . . . An' as for forgettin' him it'll be a long day before he goes out of me mind . . . We're all going to miss him an' his determined little ways; the proud way he carried himself whever he went; his love of discussin' anything you wanted to discuss; an' the happy way he ud keep his ideas an' thoughts to himself at times . . . *(He refills glasses on table, then holds one up and stares at it a moment)* And, last but not least, the way he was always fightin' an' fomentin' for the cause of Irish freedom.

MRS. LACEY. Amen.

JERRY. An' Erin Go Bragh. (MULDOON, MRS. LACEY *and* JERRY *drink.*)

MRS. MULDOON. *(Turning toward others)* Well, there can be no more arguments now about his gettin' a proper funeral.

MULDOON. No, he'll have the best we can provide him.

WILLIE. He told Mr. Bigelow he don't want any funeral. He said something about being cremated. (MULDOON, JERRY *and* MRS. LACEY *jump to their feet;* MRS. MULDOON *drops a pan she had been holding.*)

MRS. LACEY. *(Shocked)* Crematin's even worse than bein' an atheist.

MULDOON. He gives with one hand an' takes away with the other.

MRS. MULDOON. *(Crossing to* MULDOON) Oh, what will he do to us next?

MULDOON. He's goin' to make us the laughin' stock of the whole neighborhood. (WILLIE *gets up and strolls out* R.)

MRS. MULDOON. No, he ain't, because irregardless of what he wants, what he's goin' to get is a respectable funeral.

MULDOON. How the hell can you have a funeral if there's nothin' to have it with?

MRS. MULDOON. *(With finality)* I'm goin' to drive the atheism an' crematin' out of his obstinate old head without any more dilly-dallyin' . . . an' he can like it or lump it . . . Mrs. Lacey, I want you to run over after Father Malone as fast as your legs'll carry you.

MRS. LACEY. *(Starting for L. door)* Now's the time to do it before it's too late. *(She runs out.)*

MULDOON. *(Frantically calling after her)* Hey, come back here . . . *(To JERRY)* Run after her quick an' bring her back here.

MRS. MULDOON. *(Determinedly)* Jerry's goin' to stay right where he is.

MULDOON. Have you lost your wits, woman? Wasn't we just told he ain't unconscious yet? Do you want the old heathen kickin' up a terrible embarrassin' commotion?

MRS. MULDOON. He'll kick up no commotion.

MULDOON. *(Alarmed)* Supposin' he got something in his will if he ain't cremated we don't get the money?

JERRY. Couldn't you tell Bigelow he's after changin' his mind agin about bein' cremated?

MRS. MULDOON. That's just what we're goin' to tell Mr. Bigelow, but we'll not be lyin' because Uncle Hughie is goin' to change his mind. He ain't as bad as he makes out an' when he's properly talked to by the right party he's bound to see the error of his ways.

MULDOON. Provided you can get him to listen.

MRS. MULDOON. He'll listen, all right. Because you an' Jerry is goin' up an' stand by his bed an' the first funny move he makes you're goin' to grab him an' hold him down, by force if necessary.

JERRY. *(Quickly)* Don't count me in on this.

MRS. MULDOON. *(Just as quickly)* Very well, an' I won't count you in on ever comin' in this house agin either . . . take your bottle an' clear out. *(To MULDOON)* You'll have to handle him alone, Peter.

MULDOON. *(As* JERRY *edges towards* L. *door)* All right, leave him go, but by God if he goes, the funeral don't go to Danzinger and he can put that in his pipe and smoke it!

JERRY. *(Hesitating)* Who gets the funeral or who don't get it ain't worryin' me. It's the moral side I'm thinkin' about.

MULDOON. All I want to know, are you with me or agin me? (JERRY *is undecided as he stares first at* MULDOON, *then apprehensively up at ceiling. He fidgets from one foot to the other and elaborately clears his throat a couple of times. At last he makes up his mind and edges over to table, where he shakily pours himself a stiff drink.* MULDOON *follows suit and they slowly raise their glasses. A knock offstage.)*

MRS. MULDOON. There's Father Malone . . . She certainly made good time . . . You two stand ready, an' for God's sake hide that bottle. *(She exits through door* R. JERRY *quickly pours two more drinks, then sets bottle on a chair.)*

JERRY. I don't like getting mixed up in this.

MRS. MULDOON. *(Offstage)* But are you sure he's expectin' you?

MEN'S VOICES. *(Offstage)* Yes, he is expecting us . . . Which way do we go? *(Banging begins on floor above.)* He must be upstairs . . . Come on, men. (MRS. MULDOON *hurries on through door* R.)

MULDOON. What the hell is goin' on out there?

MRS. MULDOON. It's the Presbyterians from the Hospital . . . an' they got a stretcher. *(She dashes through* C. *door.)*

MULDOON. What right they got—bustin' in here like this?

JERRY. *(Overwhelmed by his discovery)* That's why he wrote 'em the letter . . . They're takin' him away!

MULDOON. Well, by God, I'm goin' to put a stop to it . . . Go up an' see what they're up to, Jerry.

JERRY. *(Indignant)* What do you think I am—a jackass? He's your uncle . . .

MULDOON. I might lose me temper . . . I tell you—we'll both go up.

JERRY. You go up—I'll keep guard down here. (MRS. MULDOON *screams offstage; then she is heard talking to someone.)*

MRS. MULDOON. You ought to be ashamed of yourself—after all we've done for you . . . How did you ever think of a thing like that? (UNCLE HUGHIE *is heard mumbling; no words can be distinguished.)*

MULDOON. What's he done now to get her tha~ agitated?

MRS. MULDOON. *(Offstage)* An' you couldn't a been any better treated if it was your own home . . . You can't do this
to us . . . Do you hear me, Uncle Hughie? *(Again mumbling is heard.)*

MAN'S VOICE. *(Offstage)* We better take him down the front
way.

MULDOON. What the hell they up to now?

MAN'S VOICE. Take it easy, there.

MULDOON. They're takin' him out of the house.

JERRY. Why don't you run up an' stop 'em?

MRS. MULDOON. *(Offstage)* Why do you do this terrible thing
to us? Speak to me, Uncle Hughie . . . speak to me.

UNCLE HUGHIE. *(In a loud, croaking voice that's still got
plenty of vigor in it)* UP THE REBELS! *(Front door is
slammed.* MRS. MULDOON *enters* R.*)*

MULDOON. Has he changed the will again?

MRS. MULDOON. *(With asperity)* How do I know whether
he's changed it or not?

MULDOON. Then why was you jawin' at him?

JERRY. Was it about him being cremated?

MRS. MULDOON. He ain't goin' to be cremated . . . The old
reprobate's willin' his body to the Presbyterian Hospital so's
they can experiment on him to find out what's been ailin' him
the last ten years.

JERRY. He can't do that to us!

MRS. MULDOON. He's done it.

MULDOON. *(Flopping down on a chair)* God give me patience.
*(He knocks whiskey bottle to floor. Both men make a dive
for bottle and collide. Whiskey continues to flow out of bottle onto the floor.)*

MULDOON. *(Grabbing bottle)* Hurry up an' get a pot an' a
rag. *(*JERRY *rushes over to shelves, grabs a rag and a pot,
runs back to* MULDOON *and hands him pot. Just as they start
mopping up spilled whiskey there is loud knocking offstage.)*

MRS. MULDOON. Oh, my goodness, there's Father Malone!

MULDOON. *(Turning his head)* What do we do now?

JERRY. Hold the pot steady.

MRS. LACEY. *(Shouting offstage)* Open up in there . . . will

yous? . . . It's me and Father Malone . . . *(Banging continues.)*
MULDOON. What'll we say to him?
MRS. MULDOON. *(In a hoarse whisper)* Be quiet an' he'll think we're not home and go about his business.
MULDOON. But Mrs. Lacey'll tell him we sent her.
JERRY. Will you hold the pot steady?
MRS. MULDOON. Quiet.
MRS. LACEY. *(Offstage)* Father Malone's here . . . Open the door . . . Do you hear me . . . *(Banging now reaches a crescendo.)*

CURTAIN

[END OF PLAY]

HAND PROPERTY LIST

HOPE IS THE THING WITH FEATHERS

2 Handkerchiefs (one for Oscar, one for Charlie)
Cloth tobacco bag for Charlie
String with corks for Doc
String with potato for Doc
Sack of corn for Doc
Pieces of newspaper for Doc
Duck feathers for Doc
Bundle (brown paper tied with heavy cord) for Joe
Jack knife for Joe
Newspapers for Nelson
Newspapers for Steve
Newspapers for Oscar
Rubber bands for Oscar

HOME LIFE OF A BUFFALO

Food in icebox
Steamer trunk
Tray (on small table U.R.)
Empty soda bottle (on small table U.R.)
3 Plates, cups, saucers, spoons, knives, forks (on small table U.R.)
5 Glasses (on small table U.R.)
3 Saucepans of varying sizes (2 on stove, 1 on small table U.R.)
Wardrobe trunk (U.R.C.) open
Night-clothes for Joe (hanging in wardrobe trunk)
Night-clothes for Josey (hanging in wardrobe trunk)
Table-cloth (folded in top drawer, wardrobe trunk)
Coins (on top of ice-box)
Lamp (D.L.)
2 School books (on table C.)
Ukelele (on table C.)

Shopping bag for Josey
Box of Corn flakes (in shopping bag)
2 Cans of vegetables (in shopping bag)
Container of milk (in shopping bag)
Loaf of bread (in shopping bag)
Sheet music, "Dirty Hands!" for Eddie D.R.
Special shoes in paper sack for Eddie D.R.
Contract for Eddie D.R.
Handkerchief for Eddie D.R.
Large wooden basket for Molly D.L.
Several packages in wooden basket
Bottle of Scotch in wooden basket
Napkin covering contents of wooden basket
American flags on sticks for Otto D.L.
Bottle of soda for Joe D.R.

GONE TOMORROW

Cover on dining table
2 Cups, saucers, and spoons on buffet U.R.
Cream pitcher and sugar bowl on buffet U.R.
Teapot on buffet U.R.
Whiskey bottle on buffet U.R.
4 Shot glasses on buffet U.R.

Tea-tray on buffet U.R.
Cardigan jacket with pipe in right pocket on clothes tree D.L.
Newspaper for Muldoon
Comic book for Willie
Pint whiskey bottle for Jerry
Calling card for Bigelow

NEW PLAYS

★ **THE CIDER HOUSE RULES, PARTS 1 & 2 by Peter Parnell, adapted from the novel by John Irving.** Spanning eight decades of American life, this adaptation from the Irving novel tells the story of Dr. Wilbur Larch, founder of the St. Cloud's, Maine orphanage and hospital, and of the complex father-son relationship he develops with the young orphan Homer Wells. "...luxurious digressions, confident pacing...an enterprise of scope and vigor..." *–NY Times.* "...The fact that I can't wait to see Part 2 only begins to suggest just how good it is..." *–NY Daily News.* "...engrossing...an odyssey that has only one major shortcoming: It comes to an end." *–Seattle Times.* "...outstanding...captures the humor, the humility...of Irving's 588-page novel..." *–Seattle Post-Intelligencer.* [9M, 10W, doubling, flexible casting] PART 1 ISBN: 0-8222-1725-2 PART 2 ISBN: 0-8222-1726-0

★ **TEN UNKNOWNS by Jon Robin Baitz.** An iconoclastic American painter in his seventies has his life turned upside down by an art dealer and his ex-boyfriend. "...breadth and complexity...a sweet and delicate harmony rises from the four cast members...Mr. Baitz is without peer among his contemporaries in creating dialogue that spontaneously conveys a character's social context and moral limitations..." *–NY Times.* "...darkly funny, brilliantly desperate comedy...TEN UNKNOWNS vibrates with vital voices." *–NY Post.* [3M, 1W] ISBN: 0-8222-1826-7

★ **BOOK OF DAYS by Lanford Wilson.** A small-town actress playing St. Joan struggles to expose a murder. "...[Wilson's] best work since *Fifth of July*...An intriguing, prismatic and thoroughly engrossing depiction of contemporary small-town life with a murder mystery at its core...a splendid evening of theater..." *–Variety.* "...fascinating...a densely populated, unpredictable little world." *–St. Louis Post-Dispatch.* [6M, 5W] ISBN: 0-8222-1767-8

★ **THE SYRINGA TREE by Pamela Gien.** Winner of the 2001 Obie Award. A breathtakingly beautiful tale of growing up white in apartheid South Africa. "Instantly engaging, exotic, complex, deeply shocking...a thoroughly persuasive transport to a time and a place...stun[s] with the power of a gut punch..." *–NY Times.* "Astonishing...affecting ...[with] a dramatic and heartbreaking conclusion...A deceptive sweet simplicity haunts THE SYRINGA TREE..." *–A.P.* [1W (or flexible cast)] ISBN: 0-8222-1792-9

★ **COYOTE ON A FENCE by Bruce Graham.** An emotionally riveting look at capital punishment. "The language is as precise as it is profane, provoking both troubling thought and the occasional cheerful laugh...will change you a little before it lets go of you." *–Cincinnati CityBeat.* "...excellent theater in every way..." *–Philadelphia City Paper.* [3M, 1W] ISBN: 0-8222-1738-4

★ **THE PLAY ABOUT THE BABY by Edward Albee.** Concerns a young couple who have just had a baby and the strange turn of events that transpire when they are visited by an older man and woman. "An invaluable self-portrait of sorts from one of the few genuinely great living American dramatists...rockets into that special corner of theater heaven where words shoot off like fireworks into dazzling patterns and hues." *–NY Times.* "An exhilarating, wicked...emotional terrorism." *–NY Newsday.* [2M, 2W] ISBN: 0-8222-1814-3

★ **FORCE CONTINUUM by Kia Corthron.** Tensions among black and white police officers and the neighborhoods they serve form the backdrop of this discomfiting look at life in the inner city. "The creator of this intense...new play is a singular voice among American playwrights...exceptionally eloquent..." *–NY Times.* "...a rich subject and a wise attitude." *–NY Post.* [6M, 2W, 1 boy] ISBN: 0-8222-1817-8

DRAMATISTS PLAY SERVICE, INC.
440 Park Avenue South, New York, NY 10016 212-683-8960 Fax 212-213-1539
postmaster@dramatists.com www.dramatists.com

NEW PLAYS

★ A LESSON BEFORE DYING by Romulus Linney, based on the novel by Ernest J. Gaines. An innocent young man is condemned to death in backwoods Louisiana and must learn to die with dignity. "The story's wrenching power lies not in its outrage but in the almost inexplicable grace the characters must muster as their only resistance to being treated like lesser beings." —*The New Yorker.* "Irresistable momentum and a cathartic explosion...a powerful inevitability." —*NY Times.* [5M, 2W] ISBN: 0-8222-1785-6

★ BOOM TOWN by Jeff Daniels. A searing drama mixing small-town love, politics and the consequences of betrayal. "...a brutally honest, contemporary foray into classic themes, exploring what moves people to lie, cheat, love and dream. By BOOM TOWN's climactic end there are no secrets, only bare truth." —*Oakland Press.* "...some of the most electrifying writing Daniels has ever done..." —*Ann Arbor News.* [2M, 1W] ISBN: 0-8222-1760-0

★ INCORRUPTIBLE by Michael Hollinger. When a motley order of medieval monks learns their patron saint no longer works miracles, a larcenous, one-eyed minstrel shows them an outrageous new way to pay old debts. "A lightning-fast farce, rich in both verbal and physical humor." —*American Theatre.* "Everything fits snugly in this funny, endearing black comedy...an artful blend of the mock-formal and the anachronistically breezy...A piece of remarkably dexterous craftsmanship." —*Philadelphia Inquirer.* "A farcical romp, scintillating and irreverent." —*Philadelphia Weekly.* [5M, 3W] ISBN: 0-8222-1787-2

★ CELLINI by John Patrick Shanley. Chronicles the life of the original "Renaissance Man," Benvenuto Cellini, the sixteenth-century Italian sculptor and man-about-town. Adapted from the autobiography of Benvenuto Cellini, translated by J. Addington Symonds. "[Shanley] has created a convincing Cellini, not neglecting his dark side, and a trim, vigorous, fast-moving show." —*BackStage.* "Very entertaining...With brave purpose, the narrative undermines chronology before untangling it...touching and funny..." —*NY Times.* [7M, 2W (doubling)] ISBN: 0-8222-1808-9

★ PRAYING FOR RAIN by Robert Vaughan. Examines a burst of fatal violence and its aftermath in a suburban high school. "Thought provoking and compelling." —*Denver Post.* "Vaughan's powerful drama offers hope and possibilities." —*Theatre.com.* "[The play] doesn't put forth compact, tidy answers to the problem of youth violence. What it does offer is a compelling exploration of the forces that influence an individual's choices, and of the proverbial lifelines—be they familial, communal, religious or political—that tragically slacken when society gives in to apathy, fear and self-doubt..." —*Westword.* "...a symphony of anger..." —*Gazette Telegraph.* [4M, 3W] ISBN: 0-8222-1807-0

★ GOD'S MAN IN TEXAS by David Rambo. When a young pastor takes over one of the most prestigious Baptist churches from a rip-roaring old preacher-entrepreneur, all hell breaks loose. "...the pick of the litter of all the works at the Humana Festival..." —*Providence Journal.* "...a wealth of both drama and comedy in the struggle for power..." —*LA Times.* "...the first act is so funny...deepens in the second act into a sobering portrait of fear, hope and self-delusion..." —*Columbus Dispatch.* [3M] ISBN: 0-8222-1801-1

★ JESUS HOPPED THE 'A' TRAIN by Stephen Adly Guirgis. A probing, intense portrait of lives behind bars at Rikers Island. "...fire-breathing...whenever it appears that JESUS is settling into familiar territory, it slides right beneath expectations into another, fresher direction. It has the courage of its intellectual restlessness...[JESUS HOPPED THE 'A' TRAIN] has been written in flame." —*NY Times.* [4M, 1W] ISBN: 0-8222-1799-6

DRAMATISTS PLAY SERVICE, INC.
440 Park Avenue South, New York, NY 10016 212-683-8960 Fax 212-213-1539
postmaster@dramatists.com   www.dramatists.com

NEW PLAYS

★ **THE CREDEAUX CANVAS by Keith Bunin.** A forged painting leads to tragedy among friends. "There is that moment between adolescence and middle age when being disaffected looks attractive. Witness the enduring appeal of Prince Hamlet, Jake Barnes and James Dean, on the stage, page and screen. Or, more immediately, take a look at the lithe young things in THE CREDEAUX CANVAS..." –*NY Times.* "THE CREDEAUX CANVAS is the third recent play about painters...it turned out to be the best of the lot, better even than most plays about non-painters." –*NY Magazine.* [2M, 2W] ISBN: 0-8222-1838-0

★ **THE DIARY OF ANNE FRANK by Frances Goodrich and Albert Hackett, newly adapted by Wendy Kesselman.** A transcendently powerful new adaptation in which Anne Frank emerges from history a living, lyrical, intensely gifted young girl. "Undeniably moving. It shatters the heart. The evening never lets us forget the inhuman darkness waiting to claim its incandescently human heroine." –*NY Times.* "A sensitive, stirring and thoroughly engaging new adaptation." –*NY Newsday.* "A powerful new version that moves the audience to gasps, then tears." –*A.P.* "One of the year's ten best." – *Time Magazine.* [5M, 5W, 3 extras] ISBN: 0-8222-1718-X

★ **THE BOOK OF LIZ by David Sedaris and Amy Sedaris.** Sister Elizabeth Donderstock makes the cheese balls that support her religious community, but feeling unappreciated among the Squeamish, she decides to try her luck in the outside world. "...[a] delightfully off-key, off-color hymn to clichés we all live by, whether we know it or not." –*NY Times.* "Good-natured, goofy and frequently hilarious..." –*NY Newsday.* "...[THE BOOK OF LIZ] may well be the world's first Amish picaresque...hilarious..." –*Village Voice.* [2M, 2W (doubling, flexible casting to 8M, 7W)] ISBN: 0-8222-1827-5

★ **JAR THE FLOOR by Cheryl L. West.** A quartet of black women spanning four generations makes up this hilarious and heartwarming dramatic comedy. "...a moving and hilarious account of a black family sparring in a Chicago suburb..." –*NY Magazine.* "...heart-to-heart confrontations and surprising revelations...first-rate..." –*NY Daily News.* "...unpretentious good feelings...bubble through West's loving and humorous play..." –*Star-Ledger.* "...one of the wisest plays I've seen in ages...[from] a master playwright." –*USA Today.* [5W] ISBN: 0-8222-1809-7

★ **THIEF RIVER by Lee Blessing.** Love between two men over decades is explored in this incisive portrait of coming to terms with who you are. "Mr. Blessing unspools the plot ingeniously, skipping back and forth in time as the details require...an absorbing evening." –*NY Times.* "...wistful and sweet-spirited..." –*Variety.* [6M] ISBN: 0-8222-1839-9

★ **THE BEGINNING OF AUGUST by Tom Donaghy.** When Jackie's wife abruptly and mysteriously leaves him and their infant daughter, a pungently comic reevaluation of suburban life ensues. "Donaghy holds a cracked mirror up to the contemporary American family, anatomizing its frailties and miscommunications in fractured language that can be both funny and poignant." –*The Philadelphia Inquirer.* "...[A] sharp, eccentric new comedy. Pungently funny...fresh and precise..." –*LA Times.* [3M, 2W] ISBN: 0-8222-1786-4

★ **OUTSTANDING MEN'S MONOLOGUES 2001–2002 and OUTSTANDING WOMEN'S MONOLOGUES 2001–2002 edited by Craig Pospisil.** Drawn exclusively from Dramatists Play Service publications, these collections for actors feature over fifty monologues each and include an enormous range of voices, subject matter and characters. MEN'S ISBN: 0-8222-1821-6 WOMEN'S ISBN: 0-8222-1822-4

DRAMATISTS PLAY SERVICE, INC.
440 Park Avenue South, New York, NY 10016 212-683-8960 Fax 212-213-1539
postmaster@dramatists.com www.dramatists.com